HENRY M. STANLEY:
The Man from Africa

Soldier, sailor, newspaper correspondent, explorer, pauper, rich man, deserter, idolized hero—Henry Morton Stanley was all these things. Probably no man ever led a more harrowing, venturesome life than the discoverer of the lost Dr. Livingstone in the heart of Africa. In a swiftly paced narrative, author Robert Edmond Alter tells the story of Stanley, from his impoverished childhood in a British workhouse to his creation of an African empire.

*Jacket design and maps
by Steele Savage*

HENRY M. STANLEY:

The Man from Africa

By Robert Edmond Alter

WILDSIDE PRESS

To
Byron Farwell
whose fine biography *The Man Who Presumed*
inspired this book

Contents

Preface *11*
1. Child of the Dark Star *13*
2. The Boy Nobody Wanted *19*
3. The First Field of Glory *27*
4. In Search of a Goal *35*
5. Adventure in Abyssinia *43*
6. "Find Livingstone!" *51*
7. Needle in a Haystack *59*
8. Stanley and Livingstone *71*
9. Hero's Return *79*
10. The Way to Lualaba *91*
11. Cannibal Country *101*
12. The Empire Builder *113*
13. The Region of Horror *121*
14. The Way Back *133*
15. The Last Trek *141*
16. "Enough" *149*

Acknowledgments and Bibliography *154*
Index *156*

THE MAN FROM AFRICA

What is in the power of human nature to do, I will do.
                                    HENRY M. STANLEY

Preface

"Dr. Livingstone, I presume?" were the four famous words spoken by the man who called himself Henry Morton Stanley, and the world has never forgotten them.

The world has, however, forgotten nearly everything else about this remarkable adventurer and journalist who founded an empire in Africa; and there is a great deal of information concerning this enigmatic man that the world never even knew. To begin with, his name was not Henry M. Stanley . . .

He was born on January 28, 1841, in northern Wales, Great Britain, and he was baptized John Rowlands. He never saw his father, who had vanished into America before he was born, and he barely knew his mother, who had abandoned him as an infant and gone off to London. Young John was left in the care of

Preface

his grandfather, a broken old man who lived in Denbigh with his two grown sons. The old gentleman died when John was four years old and he became the dependent of his two uncles.

Little John Rowlands' trials and tribulations were only beginning.

The two uncles had no love for the unwanted boy and they soon pawned him off on a family named Price, paying the Prices the handsome sum of 35 cents a week for young John's bed and board. This arrangement lasted nearly two years, and then the penurious uncles suddenly stopped sending the weekly stipend.

The Prices felt they had been left holding the bag. Why should they be responsible for a little boy who did not belong to them? They put their heads together to see what they could do about it. They were simple, hard-working people; they could not have been expected to realize that the boy would become Africa's greatest explorer.

Note: All the conversations in this book are quoted from Stanley's own writings.

1. Child of the Dark Star

IN 1847 Dick Price, the grown son of the couple who were keeping little John Rowlands, told young John that he was going to take him to the town of Ffynnon Beuno to visit his Aunt Mary. This prospect pleased the little boy and he went along with his friend quite trustingly. But he never saw his aunt, because Dick had deceived him.

The long dusty walk finally ended before a great stone cube of a building with small windows like dark eyes. A sturdy iron-barred fence surrounded the grim place. The forbidding aspect of the looming building made little John try to pull back instinctively, but Dick held him firmly by the hand as he pulled the bell cord beside the massive door.

The door swung open with a painful creak and an angular, dour-faced man glared down at the trembling boy. Without a word of warning he made a sudden snatch at little John, caught him by the wrist, and yanked him into the gloomy hallway. Terrified, John screamed and struggled and cried out for Dick to help him. But Dick did not. The dour-faced man slammed the door, and the sunlight vanished with a crash.

The six-year-old Welsh boy, without a friend in the world, was too frightened even to whimper.

The place where the Price family had abandoned him was the St. Asaph Union Workhouse. There he would live, work, attend school and learn a trade, until he was old enough to be apprenticed out to a cobbler or mason or carpenter.

A British workhouse was a kind of prison for the very young and the very old who had no means of support. Worked and treated like helpless convicts, they were up at six every morning and set to scrubbing the floors, sweeping the yards, and hoeing the rubbly fields. For youngsters there also were lessons in the classroom. They were fed a sparse meal of bread, gruel and potatoes and were locked in their dingy dormitories every night at eight. Neither their diet nor their harsh regimen ever varied—fourteen hours a day, six days a week.

An ex-miner named James Francis was the schoolmaster. He had lost one of his hands in an accident, and this had embittered him and made him a brutal tyrant. Reading and writing catechisms and reciting Bible verses were considered an adequate education for workhouse children. Francis saw to it that they became accomplished in these matters by using a sturdy ruler on them. For the slightest infraction of any of his strict classroom rules he would beat the youths mercilessly with fist, feet, cane, or a birch stick. He gave little John a sound thrashing within the first week when the still bewildered and cowed boy mispronounced a biblical word. This was only an introduction to the many floggings John Rowlands was to receive from the hand of the warped schoolmaster.

Francis was finally sent to an insane asylum. Unfortunately, it was after John had left the workhouse—after he had suffered and toiled for nine long years there.

One day, a sickly boy named Willie Roberts, who was John's best chum, disappeared. Some of the workhouse boys whispered that Francis had beaten him to death.

John refused to accept the grisly rumor. He knew nothing about death and it was impossible for him to believe that his closest friend might actually be gone forever. One of the boys suggested that John sneak into the little morgue and find out for sure. He agreed and slipped into the fearsome building known as the Deadhouse.

The morgue was a chilly, dismal place with rows of long black benches. On one of the benches lay a small form covered from head to toe with a drab sheet. His heart pounding wildly, John raised the shroud with a shaking hand....

The Man from Africa

Yes, it was Willie Roberts. And he was dead. More than that—his slim pale body was covered with bruises and gashes. It was quite apparent to the horrified 11-year-old boy that his friend had been beaten to death.

Later in life he was to see scores upon scores of dead men in the most grotesque postures imaginable, everything from soldiers torn open by shells to Africans contorted by lockjaw. But this first terrifying look at stark death was an appalling experience. He crept out of the room with a heavy feeling of dread.

He was 15 when a sudden and violent incident erupted in the classroom and completely altered the course of his life. One of the desks had been scratched and Francis demanded the name of the culprit. None of the frightened boys would confess and the schoolmaster flew into an irrational rage, shouting that he would thrash every boy in the room. He ordered them to line up and strip. Systematically and savagely, he beat the abject youths one by one with his birch stick. Then he came to John Rowlands and saw that the boy had not lowered his pants.

"How is this?" Francis cried. "Not ready yet? Strip, sir, this minute! I mean to stop this abominable and barefaced lying!"

John, outraged, replied, "I did not lie, sir! I know nothing of it."

"Silence, sir!" Francis screamed. "Down with your clothes!"

"Never again!" John shouted stubbornly.

Francis grabbed John by the scruff of the neck and pitched him brutally against a bench, then jumped on him and began pounding him in the stomach.

Gasping with pain and in mortal fear for his life, John tried to break away from the enraged man. But Francis held on to him, lifted him and banged him into the bench again with a force that nearly cracked his spine.

In frantic desperation to escape, John lashed out with his foot in a blind kick. The unexpected blow caught Mr. Francis off-guard and he reeled backward, stumbled over a bench, and struck his head on the stone floor. He was unconscious.

Panting painfully, John looked at his awestruck friends. They were utterly stunned. Such a thing had never happened in the history of the workhouse. He knew he was in very serious trouble, and there seemed to be only one thing he could do about it. Without a penny in his pockets or even a coat on his back, he climbed over the wall and started to run.

He did not suspect that he was running down a long, adventurous path.

2. The Boy Nobody Wanted

A CALLOUS world greeted lonely 15-year-old John Rowlands. Penniless, hungry, thinly garbed, he went to the home of his father's father.

Grandfather Rowlands was a well-to-do farmer with a self-righteous face and miserly heart. Dourly, he listened as John described his predicament. The old man's reply was short: Get out and stay out!

His two uncles told him the same thing. Finally, in desperate straits, he turned to his cousin Moses Owen, who ran a private boys' school in Brynford. Moses did not really want to help him, but he did offer to give his young cousin bed and board if John would work in the school as an assistant. The understanding seemed to be that John might someday become a full-fledged teacher. The homeless boy accepted the job gratefully.

The Man from Africa

At first John thought he finally had found a home. He liked his duties and, having an inquiring mind, he was delighted with the information the school's library offered him. He soon developed an avid interest in history and geography, subjects which had been deemed unnecessary in the workhouse schoolroom. It was at Brynford that he saw his first map.

Then his past caught up with him.

The pupils discovered he had no parents and was a workhouse boy. They began to ridicule him. Worse, it soon became apparent that Moses was tiring of the responsibility of supporting him. His cousin also began to berate him in an effort to drive him away. In the presence of the snickering students he would sneeringly suggest that John's head must be full of mud instead of brains, that he was good for nothing except to cobble paupers' boots.

Having nowhere else to go, without funds or the proper training for a trade, John grimly stuck to the school for nine tormented months, becoming increasingly withdrawn and bitter. Then, in 1857, Moses sent him packing to Ffynnon Beuno where Moses' mother, Mary, lived.

Aunt Mary, in turn, quickly delivered him into the hands of his Aunt Maria and Uncle Tom in Liverpool. Uncle Tom made boisterous promises. Why of course he could find his nephew a job! The best position in town, no less!

He found nothing. John, having now exhausted his entire gamut of relatives, began to walk the bustling streets of the seaport, looking for posted signs that read "Boy Wanted."

He found a job in a haberdashery: 14 hours a day, six days a week for five shillings—about 70 cents for 84 hours of work. He was let go in two months because the owner wanted a bigger and stronger boy.

John returned to the streets.

A butcher gave him a job carrying fresh meat from the shop down to the busy docks in a wheelbarrow. The 16-year-old boy was enthralled by the lofty ships that crowded the waterfront. He began to envision himself as a sailor roaming the seas and visiting the exotic lands he had read about.

One day after delivering meat to the packet ship *Windermere*, he entered the aftercabin to present the butcher's bill to the captain. The spacious and ornate cabin was a masterpiece of joinerwork which awed John.

The captain studied him calculatingly and said, "I see you admire my cabin. Would you like to live in it? How would you like to sail in this ship?"

"But I know nothing of the sea, sir," John replied.

The captain brushed his statement aside. He would ship John as cabin boy for five dollars a month. They were to sail for New Orleans in three days. What did he say to that?

John thought about it. Great Britain, to say the least, had not been kind to him. So why shouldn't he try his luck in a more promising land? He agreed to sail as cabin boy aboard the *Windermere*.

The Man from Africa

Five days before Christmas John lay in his bunk in the forecastle of the *Windermere*, groaning with seasickness. He was on his way to a new land, a new life—but at the moment he wished he could curl up and die.

He was allowed to lie in his tossing bunk for three days. Then a blasphemous mate hauled him topside, shoved a holystone at him, and ordered him to scrub the deck white.

Bewildered, weakened by excessive retching, John dropped to his knees and began to scrub the rolling deck. When he protested that the captain had signed him on as cabin boy, the old salts laughed and told him that was the captain's trick to ship deckhands cheap. He would sign on green hands with a false promise, work and bully them into jumping ship at the first port, and then keep their wages for himself. It was an old dodge.

"Ride 'em, drive 'em, haze 'em," was the captain's method of working a crew aboard his ship. The would-be cabin boy never did see the inside of the captain's quarters again. He scrubbed decks, reefed sails, manned braces, calked seams, spliced lines, mended sails, and worked in pitch and paint up to his elbows—all to a roaring tune of profanity and the constant *whack whack* of a stinging rope's end.

It was the workhouse all over again—bad food and worse treatment. And it lasted for six long harrowing weeks. Then the *Windermere* raised America.

The Boy Nobody Wanted

John was delighted by his first glimpse of New Orleans. That night he stuffed his few belongings into a small duffel bag and jumped ship.

He spent his first night in America on the Mississippi levee, bedding down in a labyrinth of piled cotton bales. Early the next morning he started looking for work—and soon learned that Negro slaves filled most of the jobs for which his meager training might have suited him. Discouraged and hungry, John approached a grocery store thinking he would make one last try at employment.

A middle-aged man sat on the porch reading a newspaper. He had thin white hair and deep lines around the mouth and eyes—an expression of wearied kindliness. His name was Henry Morton Stanley. John looked at the mild gentleman for a moment and decided to speak to him. It was as if fate had arranged this chance meeting.

"Do you want a boy, sir?" he asked hopefully.

Mr. Stanley looked up with a start. "What did you say?"

"I want some work, sir. I asked if you wanted a boy."

Mr. Stanley folded his newspaper, studied the haggard youth for a moment, then asked him his name, where he had come from, and about his education. Apparently satisfied with John's answers, he proceeded to buy him a meal and a haircut.

John's benefactor was an agent in mercantile goods, serving as middleman between the New Orleans merchants and the Mississippi River planters. He took John to a general store and introduced him to James Speake, the owner, who gave him a job as a clerk at five dollars a week—a princely sum to the youth.

John did well in Speake's store and soon was raised to 25 dollars a month. More important, Mr. Stanley had a parental affection for the lonely Welsh boy and took him to his home in New Orleans and introduced him to his wife—a kindly, but very ill woman.

When Mr. Stanley was away from home, John spent as much time as he could with the ailing Mrs. Stanley. Learning that she was dying, he quit his job at the store in order to be with her during her last few days. He was by her bed when she died.

Mr. Stanley was in St. Louis when his wife died. John booked passage on a steamboat to join him there. Arriving at the Planters' Hotel, he learned that Mr. Stanley had already departed for New Orleans.

Broke and stranded in a strange city, John spent ten days searching for work, but to no avail. Then, by chance, he found a job as a cook's boy on a flatboat bound for New Orleans.

Mr. Stanley, grief-stricken over his wife's death, was overjoyed to have John back.

They spent the next three years traveling the length of the great Mississippi, buying and selling goods and enjoying the rollicking river life.

One misty night as John and Mr. Stanley were traveling downriver on a big steamboat, a thief broke into the cabin where Mr. Stanley was asleep. John, seeing him, leaped for him, and the thief slashed out with a bowie knife. The blade ripped John's coat but missed his skin, and the thief escaped in the confusion.

Mr. Stanley, moved by John's devotion, told him, "I promise to take you for my son . . . and in the future you are to bear my name, Henry Stanley."

3. The First Field of Glory

WHEN Mr. Stanley had to go to Havana, he sent his foster son to Cypress Bend, Arkansas, to work on a cotton plantation owned by a Major Ingham. It was a sad parting for young Stanley, who did not know they would never meet again.

The Ingham plantation was in a wilderness along the Saline River. Stanley liked Major and Mrs. Ingham, but not the plantation overseer—a brutish braggart who tyrannized the helpless slaves.

One day Stanley was helping the major's slaves clear land for cotton when two Negroes struggled by him, bearing a heavy log on their shoulders. Suddenly, without provocation, the overseer's whip whisked over Stanley's shoulder and landed with a sickening crack on the bare back of one of the laboring Negroes. Both slaves lost their grip and the huge log crashed to the ground.

Outraged by the unwarranted cruelty, Stanley cursed the overseer, then returned to the house and told Major Ingham what had happened. Ingham, unperturbed, told Stanley that the overseer had every right to whip the fieldhands.

Stanley disagreed vehemently. He had seen enough brutality in the workhouse and aboard the *Windermere* to last him the rest of his life. Angrily he left the plantation and got himself a job clerking in a local store.

It was a historic day in American history—April 12, 1861. Fort Sumter had been fired upon and the Civil War had begun.

Stanley knew very little about American politics. He saw no reason why he should become personally involved in a civil war. The people of Cypress Bend thought otherwise, however. When Stanley did not join the men flocking to the Confederate Army, he received a package containing chicken feathers wrapped in a lady's petticoat.

His fiery pride was outraged. If they were going to call him a coward, then he would prove them wrong! He walked out of the store and joined a group of volunteers who were embarking on a steamboat bound for Little Rock.

Stanley was sworn into the Confederate Army at the induction camp. There was no problem about a physical examination. An officer glanced at him and asked if he were physically fit. When Stanley said yes, he was

The First Field of Glory

taken at his word. He was enrolled in the 6th Arkansas Regiment, issued a flintlock musket and a new gray uniform. He then bought himself a Colt pistol and a bowie knife and tramped off to his quarters feeling like a 20-year-old warrior.

But for the next nine months the nearest he came to war was to march and drill, sharpen his bayonet, and clean his musket.

It seemed to him that the Confederacy didn't know just what to do with the 6th Arkansas. His regiment was constantly being shuttled about the South—from Arkansas to Georgia, to Kentucky, to Tennessee, and finally to Alabama. Then, late in March 1862, the regiment was put on a train and sent to Corinth, Mississippi, to be attached to General Albert Sidney Johnston's army.

Johnston, a foxy fighter, knew that General Ulysses S. Grant was massing his Union troops at Pittsburg Landing on the Tennessee River with the intention of demolishing the rebels at Corinth. So Johnston decided to get in the first punch. His 40,000 Rebs would hit Grant's 50,000 Yanks with a surprise attack.

On April 4, drums rolled, bugles shrilled, and Stanley's regiment swung out of Corinth singing "Dixie." They knew they were going into combat. They did not know it was to be one of the bloodiest ever fought: the Battle of Shiloh.

At dawn on April 6, Stanley was standing at ease in a three-mile line of excited Confederates, waiting for the command to move up and attack. The 6th Arkansas was armed with obsolete flintlocks and the ammunition was rolled in cartridge paper which contained powder, a round ball, and three buckshot. The Yankees were armed with rapid-loading Enfields and Minié rifles.

At the command to advance, the long gray line swayed forward. Before the troops had gone 500 paces they heard desultory firing up front. Soon a roar of musketry broke from the regiment on their left, followed by a terrific volley on their right. The trees overhead began to rain twigs and leaves and the branches jumped and hummed.

A nervous excitement trembled through the line as the men surged forward, picking up speed, beginning to lose alignment. Someone yelled he could see the Yankees.

Stanley felt he was blasting at shadows. Then, still firing as he advanced, he saw little globes of pearly smoke spurting from a long line of blue soldiers. Suddenly frightened, he glanced around at his comrades and was relieved to see all were pale and solemn. They continued to advance, step by step, loading and firing feverishly. Some 20,000 muskets were being fired and men were dropping everywhere in the uproar.

The tattered gray line began to run in a scrambling charge. At first the blue line appeared inclined to await their attack. Then the oncoming Confederates cut loose with a rebel yell—"*Yeee-yooo-yooo-wooo!*"—and all order was lost as the screaming Rebs piled wildly into the Yankee camp. It was too much for the bluecoats, who took off helter-skelter.

Stanley and his comrades, pausing for breath in the sprawling tent camp, thought the battle was about over. But it was only a prologue to many deadly struggles that took place that day. They were ordered to advance again, and the next Stanley knew they were running into a furious storm of bullets.

The world seemed to be bursting into fragments around him. Cannon and rifle, canister and minié balls were belching, roaring, humming and ripping. The air was alive with thousands of buzzing wasps. A huge tree lay on the ground, and Stanley and a dozen others flung themselves behind it for shelter.

With the incessant whack, slap, snip and hum of bullets beating a furious tattoo on the outer face of the protective log, Stanley marveled that any of them could live through the vicious rain of death. Many didn't.

It was ten A.M. when the Rebs poured through the second line of Yankee tents. Stanley started to slow down. He had to catch his breath or he would fall. Suddenly a sledgehammer blow slammed his stomach and he hit the ground, gasping with shock and pain.

Realizing he wasn't dead, he sat up and inspected himself. A minié ball had cracked his belt buckle, knocking the wind out of him but leaving him uninjured.

He remembered he hadn't eaten since four A.M. and now he was ravenous. Sitting where he was, he ate wolfishly from his haversack. Then he started to follow in the corpse-littered wake of his regiment.

For a time he stumbled through the bloody thickets alone or in the company of other Rebs who had also lost contact with their units. Around noon he entered a woodland glade where more than 1,000 men lay dead —some his comrades. Appalled, he trudged away dazedly. It was the first field of glory he had seen in his life, and he was beginning to suspect that glory was a glittering lie.

He located what was left of the 6th Arkansas an hour later. The men were sprawled behind trees, logs and in hollows, banging away at the Yankees who were slowly being pushed back to the river bank.

Johnston had been shot from his horse and had bled to death. The Confederate attack began to lose its momentum. Stanley was in a daze. His lips were caked with powder and grime from tearing the paper cartridges, his canteen was dry, his food gone, and the protracted excitement of the dawn-to-dusk battle had unstrung his nerves.

The long bloody day dragged into twilight. Just before dark the 6th Arkansas moved up again and captured another Yankee camp. No one had the strength left to go another foot or fire another round. Stanley crawled into a sagging tent and discovered a box of biscuits and a canteen of molasses. He stuffed himself and fell asleep on some nameless Yankee's blankets.

The First Field of Glory

A torrential rain turned the ghastly battlefield into a quagmire that night. Daybreak showed the weary Confederates that Grant had been a busy man. He had reinforced his shattered lines during the night, and now was set to make a counterattack through the wet woods.

Stanley fell in with his company. There were only 50 left, and they were ordered to form a skirmish line and advance. Stanley moved out more quickly than was prudent. The next he knew he was in a large open field. Spotting a small hollow in the weeds about 20 yards ahead, he made a dash for it, believing his company was behind him.

He stumbled into the hollow and began firing and reloading. The oncoming Yankees came closer—more and more of them. Glancing around he saw with horror that he was the only Reb soldier in the field!

A dozen Yanks swarmed upon him, yelling at him to surrender. He dropped his empty weapon and dazedly raised his hands. Somebody jabbed a bayonet in the small of his back and told him to start marching. Two Yankees led him back to the rear of the Union lines.

The war he did not understand and had not wanted to join suddenly seemed to be over.

4. In Search of a Goal

THE NEXT day Stanley was shoved aboard a steamboat crowded to the rails with haggard Confederate prisoners and transported to St. Louis. There they were locked in a schoolhouse for four days, then were herded into boxcars like cattle and sent to Camp Douglas, a P.O.W. camp near Chicago.

To Stanley and his fellow sufferers Camp Douglas was like an enormous slave pen. Disease was rampant and there were no medical supplies of any sort for the prisoners. Any form of hygiene was unheard of and the open sinks in the center of the camp were foul beyond belief. The very soil reeked with miasmatic accretions and hordes of vermin crawled everywhere. The food at best was slop that barely would sustain life.

There were 300 dirty, apathetic men in Stanley's barracks. Some were raving mad, others quietly insane. Many spent hours doing nothing but picking lice from their clothes. A few simply sat and stared bleakly at the grubby floor, day after day, month after month. Of the 7,500 Reb prisoners crammed in the compound, over 1,000 suffered the horrors of scurvy and all knew the agonies of dysentery. They died by the scores.

When elected to draw the daily rations for his barracks, Stanley made friends with the commissary director and they soon began to engage in long political discussions. Until this time Stanley had never heard the North's viewpoint on the war, and he began to suspect he had been fighting on the wrong side. The director told him that if he would agree to abandon the Confederacy and join the Union Army he would promptly be released from Camp Douglas.

At first the idea of becoming a turncoat was repugnant to Stanley, but the more he thought about it the more it began to appeal. In a sense he had been pressured into a war he did not understand, into joining a side that was actually against his principles. Now that he had been captured, why should he die for the Confederacy as a worthless prisoner of war? At the alarming rate that men were dying in Camp Douglas he felt he had little chance of staying alive. It was a frightening thought.

He did not yet know what he wanted to become, what path he should take to achievement. All he knew was that he had a driving urge to accomplish something of tremendous importance, something that the world could remember centuries after he was gone.

IN SEARCH OF A GOAL

But a dead prisoner of war could accomplish nothing.

He agreed to the terms, was removed from Camp Douglas in June of 1862, and enlisted in the Union artillery. But he never did become a Yankee soldier. Within three days he fell sick with dysentery and was sent to the hospital at Harper's Ferry. Two weeks later he was discharged from the Union Army as unfit for military service.

On his own once again in a strange land, without a cent to his name or a friend in the world, he became an itinerant farmhand. Eventually he arrived in Baltimore and got a job on an oyster schooner.

Penny by penny he scraped together enough money to buy his passage on a ship bound for Cuba. His one thought was to find his foster father. But he was two years too late. Mr. Stanley, he learned, had died in 1861.

Without money, relatives, home or a purpose in life, he shipped out as an able-bodied seaman on a merchant brig. After crossing the Atlantic and passing through the Straits of Gibraltar, his ship was caught in a storm off Barcelona. Wind and waves took the brig apart sail by timber, leaving a sinking hulk to the mercy of the crashing seas.

Hearing the order to abandon ship, Stanley grabbed a loose plank and went over the side into the rampaging black sea. The entire crew of the wrecked brig was lost in the howling night—all except young Henry Stanley clinging leechlike to his floating plank.

In the cold, foggy light of dawn he was washed ashore on a lonely beach near Barcelona. Stark naked, he staggered from the sea and found four policemen confronting him. They demanded his identification papers!

The 22-year-old Stanley returned to America, hoping to find something—anything. In the winter of 1863 he was boarding with an insane man and his shrewish wife in Brooklyn. One night the man crept into Stanley's room with a hatchet in his hand—just to tell him that he planned to murder his wife.

Stanley took the hatchet and sat with the insane man for the rest of the night. Worn out from his ordeal, he went into the parlor in the morning and sat down to relax with a cigar. Then the wife he had saved from being butchered stamped into the room and cried at him to get out of the parlor with his filthy cigar!

The irony of the situation did not amuse the exhausted Stanley at the moment. He packed up and set out to find a more sane boardinghouse.

Down on his luck again in the summer of 1864, he enlisted in the U.S. Navy for a three-year tour of duty. He was sent to the North Atlantic Blockading Squadron and assigned to the U.S.S. *Minnesota*. In November of that year he was put in charge of the ship's log and records.

In December the fleet moved against Wilmington,

In Search of a Goal

North Carolina, where General Butler landed troops to storm Fort Fisher, which was protecting the vital Confederate seaport. Butler botched the job and had to retreat, but the U.S. fleet continued to bombard the port until Grant sent Admiral Porter and General Terry to take over. Porter proceeded to pound the fort apart with his heavy guns, and Terry led his troops ashore in an assault. The South's last seaport soon was lost.

While observing these engagements and recording them in the ship's log, Stanley discovered something about himself. He not only liked to write; he was, in fact, an excellent writer. He had a good eye for detail and a natural talent for graphically describing what he saw.

Why should he not try to do something with this talent? Perhaps it was the very thing he had been searching for all his life.

He wrote a moving eyewitness account of the land and sea attacks against Fort Fisher and sent a copy to all the major newspapers in the North. His battle stories were promptly accepted and published. Overnight he had become a free-lance journalist.

But there was a hitch. How could he continue to be a roving reporter when he was stuck in the Navy? The war which had furnished so many stirring events for the newspapers was almost over, and his enlistment was not up for another two and one half years. Right or wrong, he decided there was only one thing to do. He would desert.

The Man from Africa

In January 1865, the *Minnesota* arrived at Portsmouth, New Hampshire, to be decommissioned. Stanley and a young seaman named Louis Noe did not wait to be reassigned to a new ship and sent back to sea. On February 10 the two youths slipped away, and Stanley headed west.

The war was over and thousands of men, women and children were following the lure of the West. That vast territory had become the stage for some fascinating characters: mountain men and prospectors, bandits and rustlers, gamblers and buffalo hunters, mule skinners and wagon masters.

Stanley paid his way as a roving reporter, recording the colorful events of the brawling West and sending his stories to various Eastern newspapers.

From St. Joseph he struck across the plains, cooking prairie meals on buffalo chip fires, visiting Indians, gambling with cavalrymen, herding with cowboys, hooking onto wagon trains. On he went to Salt Lake City, and then back again: Denver, North Platte, Omaha, following the adventure trail.

In Denver in the spring of 1866, he teamed up with a young man named W. H. Cook. Together they decided to pool their resources and make an expedition down the Platte River into the Black Hawk country. It was a wild, dangerous scheme. Building a small flat-bottomed boat, they stocked it with provisions, trade trinkets and arms, and drifted down the lonely Platte.

In Search of a Goal

They never had a chance to fight heroic battles with the Indians, but twice their boat encountered sandbars and turned over, spilling men, food, weapons and trinkets into the water. It was a bedraggled pair of young men who finally arrived in Omaha. But Stanley was far from discouraged. The disastrous boat trip had given him an idea. As far as he was concerned, the West had played out its news stories. Barroom brawls, stagecoach robberies and Indian skirmishes were becoming commonplace, and he wanted to find bigger and better things. He proposed to Cook that they explore Asia.

The two young adventurers, along with Stanley's former Navy friend Louis Noe, sailed from Boston in July of 1866 and landed at Smyrna, Turkey, the following month. The expedition was ill-fated from the very beginning.

Spending the night in a small village just east of Smyrna, Louis Noe built a cookfire that set the entire village ablaze. Turkish peasants howled for the blood of the three Americans. Pacifying the villagers to some extent and at some cost, the three beat a hurried retreat into the hills. Their troubles had only begun, however.

After spending a few miserable days stumbling about in the parched underbrush, they encountered a Turk who identified himself as a guide. They followed him innocently.

Thinking they were being led into the heart of the vast Anatolia Plain, the three adventurers soon found the treacherous Turk had led them into a bandit camp.

The outlaws beat them, stripped them of their letters of credit, passports, and all of their money, which amounted to 1,200 dollars. Then the bandits turned them over to the police, who placed them under arrest as thieves!

For five nightmarish days the hapless Americans were dragged from village to village and displayed as shining examples of Turkish justice. Spat on, stoned, insulted and abused, they finally were thrown into a vermin-invested prison in Smyrna and left to rot.

Fortunately, an agent of the Imperial Ottoman Bank learned of their plight and effected their release. Stanley immediately wrote a feature story about the mishap of the expedition and sold it to an English newspaper in Turkey. An American minister stationed in Constantinople read the account and sent the three destitute adventurers enough money to buy their passage back to the United States.

Henry Stanley's initial expeditions had proved to be fiascos. But something better was in store for him.

5. Adventure in Abyssinia

STANLEY found a job as special correspondent for the Missouri *Democrat* and, in March of 1867, he was sent west to cover General Winfield Scott Hancock's campaign against Comanches and Kiowas.

It was a bloodless "war," since the Indian chiefs were willing to smoke the peace pipe and discuss treaties. Therefore, Stanley's news reports had to depend largely on human interest stories, and he made the most of it.

He wrote about a five-year-old Indian boy who had attached himself to the general. The little fellow, son of a chief who had been killed in the Sand Creek massacre, lived up to his savage father's name by drawing his knife on anyone who tried to reprimand him. He was called Wilson Graham because he had once been exhibited as a curiosity by the Wilson and Graham Circus.

The Man from Africa

The many picturesque Indian scouts who led the expedition provided Stanley with entertaining stories. Notable among these was the legendary Wild Bill Hickok who, upon being asked, told Stanley he supposed he had killed "considerably" over a hundred white men. The longhaired, rawboned plainsman took a liking to the short, stocky 26-year-old reporter, and proved to be a good friend. When a rowdy tried to pick a fight with Stanley in a saloon, Hickok quickly resolved the matter by snatching the man off the floor and pitching him headfirst across a billiard table.

That summer Stanley found time to take a trip into the Colorado mountains to try his hand at prospecting. There he found glittering nuggets lying on the ground! In a fever of excitement he stuffed his pockets and saddlebag with the gleaming ore and hurried back to his hotel. Then, selecting a choice nugget, he took it to a miner and asked his opinion. The miner told him it was a fair sample of iron pyrites. Stanley had found a bonanza of fool's gold.

When the Indian peace treaties had been signed, Stanley returned to the East and was pleased to learn that his vivid style of writing had attracted some attention. By contributing to six major newspapers, he was now earning as much as 90 dollars a week. By January of 1868 he had saved 3,000 dollars. For the first time in his life he felt wholly independent. But he had had to pay for this sense of security by practicing a rigid economy.

Security was not his goal, however. He wanted action, travel, new places, strange faces, a sense of accomplishment. Reading that the British intended to send an expeditionary force into Abyssinia to punish King Theodore, Stanley decided to go to East Africa.

Abandoning five of his newspaper jobs, he went to the New York *Herald* and asked to see James Gordon Bennett, its publisher. The thin, gray tycoon and the short, stocky young reporter sat down to discuss Stanley's proposal.

Bennett did not think there was a worthwhile story in the Abyssinian war, but he asked under what conditions Stanley would be willing to go there. Stanley told him either as a special correspondent on a straight salary, or paid by the story. If, however, the *Herald* paid him by the story, he would reserve the right to sell his stories to other newspapers as well.

Bennett said the *Herald* did not like to share its news with its competitors. But it *would* pay extremely well for exclusive stories. Had Stanley ever been abroad before? Did he know his way about on the other side of the Atlantic? Yes, Stanely assured him.

Bennett then made a proposition. The *Herald* would take Stanley on a trial basis if he would pay his own way to Abyssinia. If his stories proved to be of interest, the paper would pay him at the standard rate of its foreign correspondents.

It was a one-side gamble with the *Herald* standing to lose nothing. But Stanley was willing to accept Bennett's terms, though it would mean money out of his own pocket. Two days later he was aboard the steamer *Hecla* bound for Europe.

Landing in England, he took the first available steamer to Egypt. Upon arriving at Suez, he went to the telegraph office. There he bribed the chief telegrapher to give the stories he filed precedence over those of other campaign correspondents.

Traveling by boat, he located the British expeditionary force at Zula, a port on the Red Sea. Neither the British journalists nor the officers of the expedition wanted an American along. Stanley found himself in an uncomfortable position. Having been in a rush to catch up with the army, he arrived at Zula without a tent and with little baggage. About all he actually had were pencil, pad, and a great hairy buffalo robe in which he slept. When the army started its 400-mile march to Theodore's mountain stronghold at Magdala, Stanley called on the commanding general, Sir Robert Napier, to present his credentials and request a tent.

Sir Robert's response was so cool that Stanley left angrily. It was the same story wherever he turned; he was snubbed or ignored or icily surveyed.

The expeditionary force, in characteristic 19th century British style, moved toward the enemy in a glacial manner. Engineers went ahead to build the camps the army occupied. It was April 9 when the force finally arrived at the foot of the mountainous Magdala stronghold.

Unconcerned by the seemingly impregnable fortress

frowning down on them, the British began their attack the following day. The English and Irish regiments, ably supported by regiments of Punjabis, Beluchis and Sepoys, along with artillery, elephants, camels, horses and mules, started doggedly up the shot-racked slopes. Sir Robert and his staff maintained a position directly behind the first line of attackers.

King Theodore sent 3,500 armed Abyssinians down the hillside to shatter the redcoats. For tense moments it appeared that the spearhead of the British force had been overwhelmed as Theodore's screaming horde poured down the slope.

Sir Robert sat his horse calmly, prepared to die rather than retreat. The Abyssinians had almost reached him when the naval brigade unlimbered its battery and began lobbing rocket shells into the howling warriors. Surprised and bewildered by the rockets bursting among them, the warriors raced away under a hail of rifle fire. But their chiefs soon rallied them, and then they tried to make a flank attack on the British baggage train. Again they were outmatched, and this time they fell back in utter chaos as the King's Own 4th Foot charged them with rapid-firing Snider rifles and the veteran Sepoys swept in with leveled bayonets.

It had taken the British the better part of the day to drive the Abyssinians back up the hill. At sunset Sir Robert ordered his weary troops to retire from the field. Stanley curled up in his buffalo robe for the night and tried not to listen to the cries from the distant wounded.

In the morning he went with a captain of the 4th Foot to take a tally of the battle casualties. It would make an interesting item for his news story. They visited the field hospital first, and learned that the British losses were only 32 wounded and no deaths. Then they went out to the battlesite and found that the Abyssinians had suffered 75 wounded and 560 killed. It was quite a victory for Sir Robert.

That day King Theodore, hoping to conciliate the British, released the prisoners he had been holding and sent them to the British camp. One was the British consul in Abyssinia, who told of barbaric torture:

"Twenty Abyssinians tugged lustily on ropes tied to each of my limbs until I fainted. My shoulder blades were made to meet each other. I was doubled up until my head appeared under my thighs, and while in this painful posture, I was beaten with a whip of hippopotamus hide on my bare back until I was covered with weals, and while the blood dripped from my reeking back, I was rolled in the sand."

Sir Robert demanded the Abyssinians' unconditional surrender. Ignoring Theodore's overtures, he resumed the attack the next morning.

In the midst of the siege one of the released prisoners led Stanley into the fissured hills and showed him the stripped corpses of over 300 prisoners who had been butchered by Theodore's men and dumped into a small ravine.

Adventure in Abyssinia

Sickened by the grisly scene, Stanley was pleased to learn that Theodore was not captured alive when Magdala fell to the British that afternoon. Ironically, the king had committed suicide with a pistol which Queen Victoria had presented to him several years before.

When the triumphant army returned to Zula, Stanley requested permission to dispatch a messenger to Suez with his news story. Permission was denied. He was informed that Sir Robert would decide when to release all dispatches concerning the campaign.

Stanley was far from pleased. James Gordon Bennett ran a *daily* paper, not a monthly, and he would be outraged if he knew that his reporter was sitting on a firsthand account of a brilliant campaign.

There was only one obvious course: to reach Suez as quickly as possible. So he boarded the first embarking troopship and sailed up the Red Sea.

When the ship arrived at Suez, he was greeted by more delay: all passengers would be quarantined for five days! But Stanley knew the trick of greasing the right palm with the right amount and smuggled his story ashore to his cohort in the telegraph office.

His story was wired to London and relayed to the New York *Herald*. It not only was the first dispatch on the Abyssinian campaign; it was the *only one* to get out of the country for a long time. Minutes after his story was wired, the cable snapped between Alexandria and Malta. It was three weeks before it could be repaired.

Britain was stunned by Stanley's news scoop. He had even beaten Sir Robert's official dispatches! Bennett was so pleased that he made Stanley a permanent foreign correspondent at a salary of 2,000 dollars a year.

Stanley went to Alexandria to wait for new orders. His primary thought was that he would have to take pains to see that his second scoop was as big a success as his first. He wondered where the *Herald* would send him next.

6. "Find Livingstone!"

A RUMOR had been circulating for some time that Dr. David Livingstone, the celebrated explorer and missionary, was coming out of East Africa to return to his home in Great Britain. So Bennett instructed Stanley to proceed to Aden to try to locate and interview him.

Livingstone at that time was a 56-year-old Scot who had devoted 28 years to the exploration of Africa, trying to bring enlightenment to Africans. He had trekked up and down the Zambesi, Shire and Rouha rivers, locating and recording lakes, mountains, deserts, rivers and savage tribes. In 1865 the Royal Geographical Society commissioned him to explore the district between Lake Tanganyika and Lake Nyasa. And he had gone beyond that point to try to discover the source of the White Nile. For the past three years no direct communication had come from him. There was a growing doubt that he still was alive.

Late in 1866 some of Livingstone's Zanzibar porters had returned to the east coast of Africa, saying that the doctor was definitely dead. The Royal Geographical Society viewed this report skeptically, however, and the British Government sent an expedition to Africa to uncover proof. Livingstone was not located, but the expedition did find that his porters had told contradictory stories about his death. As a result, there was great public interest in Livingstone's fate.

Stanley arrived at Aden, the gateway to the Red Sea, in November 1868. For more than two months he waited impatiently. When it seemed apparent the report regarding Livingstone had been false, the *Herald* assigned him to cover a rebellion in Spain.

Landing at Valencia in March 1869, the young reporter found himself in the midst of a bitter civil war. Alone in a strange city, surrounded by the chaos of house-to-house fighting, he prowled the bullet-whipped streets in search of a hotel. Time and again he was accosted by soldiers with leveled bayonets and had to produce his credentials. After some hours he located a hotel.

It was on a contested street. In order to reach the lobby he would have to expose himself to a 20-foot length of deadly crossfire. He took a running leap—and made it.

It was a typical act for Stanley. His bravery was inherent. He was driven by a need to prove himself to

"Find Livingstone!"

the world. Somehow, someway, he would reach the top.

But it was not to happen in Spain. The highest position he obtained in that embattled land was to climb up to an exposed roof and lie there for 36 hours watching the rebels erect a street barricade and fight off assaults by government troops.

It was during his Spanish interlude that a friend, worrying that Stanley would drive himself into an early grave, suggested he should try to relax more, even take a well-deserved vacation. Stanley's reply might well be the key to his enigmatic personality:

"Away from work my conscience accuses me of forgetting duty, of wasting time, of forgetting my God. I cannot help that feeling. It makes me feel as though the world were sliding from under my feet. Even if I had a month's holiday, I could not take it; I would be restless, dissatisfied, gloomy, morose. To the devil with a vacation! I don't want it."

After six months of war reporting in Spain, Stanley received a puzzling telegram from the *Herald* which instructed him to proceed to Paris, and report to Bennett's son at the Grand Hotel. The reason was not stated.

On October 27, 1869, Stanley entered the hotel and was handed the most dramatic assignment in journalism.

James Gordon Bennett, Jr., was like his famous father. He was exactly Stanley's age: 28. But there was no further similarity between the two. The chief assistant of the *Herald*, who had been born a multimillionaire, and the *Herald*'s best reporter, who had been born a pauper, looked at each other. Bennett was in bed. He said:

"Who are you?"

"My name is Stanley."

Bennett told him to sit down. Then he asked, "Where do you think Livingstone is?"

"I really don't know, sir."

"Do you think he is alive?"

"He may be and he may not be."

"Well," Bennett said, "I think he is alive and that he can be found, and I am going to send you to find him."

"What! Do you really think I can find Dr. Livingstone? Do you mean me to go to Central Africa?"

"Yes, I mean that you shall go and find him wherever you may hear that he is, and to get what news you can of him. And perhaps the old man may be in want; take enough with you to help him should he require it. Of course, you will act according to your own plans, and do what you think best—*but find Livingstone!*"

Stanley was stunned by the magnitude of the assignment. He knew that finding Livingstone might well be the news story of the century—but *how* to find him, and *where*? The doctor could be anywhere from Equatoria in the north to the Cape of Good Hope in the south, an area comprising one-half of the vast conti-

"FIND LIVINGSTONE!"

nent. It would be like trying to find a needle in a haystack, a very costly needle for the *Herald*.

"Have you considered seriously the great expense you are likely to incur on account of this little journey?" he asked.

"What will it cost?"

Stanley told him that the Burton and Speke expedition to Central Africa in 1857 had cost in the neighborhood of four thousand pounds (about 20,000 dollars). Money, however, was one thing Bennett did not have to worry about.

"Well," he said, "I'll tell you what you will do. Draw a thousand pounds now, and when you have gone through that, draw another thousand, and when that is spent draw another . . . and so on. But *find Livingstone.*"

The historic meeting was over. The two young men shook hands, and Bennett said, "That is all. Good night, and God be with you."

"Good night, sir. What is in the power of human nature to do I will do."

Stanley was on his way that same night, leaving on the Marseilles express to begin a sketchy tour of the Near East. He was not at that time an explorer, only a foreign correspondent, and he made many stops along the way to put his acute powers of observation to work for the sake of his newspaper.

At Port Said he attended the grand ceremonies for the opening of the Suez Canal; then, traveling up the Nile by dhow, he reported on the marvels and mysteries of ancient Egypt. At Jerusalem he followed Christ's path to Golgotha. He went to Constantinople with the express purpose of paying back the American minister who had saved the Stanley-Cook-Noe expedition four years before. Then he wandered over the past battlefields of the Crimean War.

Along the way he studied books on African customs and previous expeditions into the continent, notably by Livingstone, Burton, Speke, Grant and Baker. Never for a moment did he dream that soon his own name would join these others and far surpass them.

While in Palestine he hired an Arab youth as an interpreter. The boy was a Christian, his name was Selim, and he was to become Stanley's most faithful follower. The next to join the party was William Farquhar, the first mate of the ship which carried Stanley and Selim across the Arabian Sea.

The little party debarked at Zanzibar on January 6, 1871, and Stanley looked up the United States consul to learn if there had been any news of Dr. Livingstone, or from the *Herald* regarding money. The answer was no on both counts. Stanley had exactly 80 dollars to his name, and Selim and Farquhar had nothing.

Rather than waste precious time waiting for orders and funds, Stanley—with the United States consul's help—borrowed what he needed on the *Herald*'s name. Originally he had thought he could outfit a safari to fit his needs for about 12,500 dollars, but it turned out to be an underestimate. The actual cost of the expedition was 20,000 dollars. He had an idea that

"Find Livingstone!"

the Bennetts would be angry when presented with the bill. Now he was too impatient to leave for the interior of Tanganyika to worry about that. Young Bennett had told him to find Livingstone, dead or alive, and by hook or crook he was going to do it.

At least 8,000 dollars of his borrowed money went for "African currency," which meant beads and brass, copper wire and colorful cloth. Beads were the most popular medium of exchange, and a problem was that each tribe was partial to a different kind of bead.

Stanley rounded up 27 *pagazis* (bearers) and 13 *askaris* (guards). All were Zanzibaris, and a few had been on other African safaris. He also had one white officer, Farquhar; one interpreter, Selim; one *kirangozi* (guide), Asmani; one captain of askaris, Bombay; one cook and a boy helper; and 17 pack donkeys.

At the last moment an English sailor named John Shaw approached Stanley. He had been the third mate on an American ship which had recently stopped at Zanzibar. Now he wanted to leave the sea and join the expedition. Stanley made the mistake of accepting the man.

On February 6, 1871, Stanley gathered together his safari and prepared to embark on Arab dhows for the mainland of Africa. Then he discovered that Farquhar and Shaw were missing. After some searching he found both drunk in a saloon and had to roust them out angrily. He would have been better off had he left them behind.

They disembarked at Bagamoyo on the coast, nearly

The Man from Africa

800 miles east of the village of Ujiji, which was situated on the eastern shore of Lake Tanganyika. The last news concerning Dr. Livingstone had come from Ujiji. That was absolutely all Stanley knew of the whereabouts of the missing missionary.

He wanted to start quickly for Ujiji, but first he had to secure more bearers. This proved to be difficult because the Arab traders he had to deal through attempted to cheat him outrageously. Thus he lost two valuable weeks haggling over terms.

His greatest concern was that the rainy season would catch them somewhere in the wilderness. The torrential rains would flood the creeks and turn the open savannas into vast quagmires. To offset this threat somewhat, he broke his expedition into six small sections and started the first few men on their way.

Forty-three exasperating days after landing in Bagamoyo, Stanley at last had enough bearers and guards to march his sixth section out of the squalid village. Asmani, the guide, led the way, carrying the American flag.

It was March 21, 1871, and he finally was on his way to find Dr. Livingstone.

7. Needle in a Haystack

THE STRUNG-OUT safari now consisted of 192 men, two horses and 27 donkeys. Its weapons consisted of one shotgun, two carbines, four rifles, eight pistols, and 24 muskets, besides a boar spear, two swords, two daggers, 24 hatchets and 24 knives.

In the beginning Stanley adopted a wise approach to his task. He resolved to put all worldly interests out of his mind and to concentrate only on his mission to find Livingstone, wherever he might be. He would forget everything he had left behind and would not fret about what lay ahead.

It was a worthy resolve, but he reckoned without the tremendous pressures of nature that Africa can wield against even a determined man's will.

The expedition trudged across great open grasslands, wading into vast seas of wavering reeds which sometimes rose ten feet high and threatened to submerge them. The heat soared to 128 degrees day after day. Bearers staggered, dropped their loads, fell to the parched earth. Some died. Others deserted at night. The deadly tsetse flies, bearers of sleeping sickness, stung the beasts of burden—and they crumpled in their tracks. Soon there were nearly six tons of supplies to be hauled by the men.

Following an old overgrown Arab caravan trail, they left every sign of civilized habitation far behind. Their path meandered through stands of stunted evergreen. Plodding feet kicked up clouds of dust under the turquoise sky. There was no sign of either wild animal or man. Sometimes they glimpsed the purple-tinted mass of the Usagara Range, shimmering in the west.

Slaglike mounds of granite loomed around them. Some looked as if giants had once tried to stack them in the shape of crenellated castles. Others had been worn by erosion into the forms of crouching animals.

Their path weaved out of the spurs, skirted the mountains, and led them into more grasslands. Then the rains came. Rivers and streams overflowed, inundating the lowlands and turning everything to muck. Men and beasts struggled desperately in the sloughs. Every rampant river became a nightmarish ordeal to ford.

Worse than the tsetse were the hordes of disease-bearing insects which the rains hatched. Stanley averaged an attack of fever twice a month.

All the infectious horrors of a torrid zone visited the

safari. Dysentery, beriberi, jungle rot, malaria and smallpox made deadly inroads. William Farquhar contracted elephantiasis; both his legs swelled gigantically. Unable to walk and in too much pain to be carried, he had to be left behind in an isolated village of the Ugogo territory.

There was nothing Stanley could do for Farquhar except to leave him a six-month stock of food and trade goods. But the former seaman died a few days after the expedition left him behind.

Determined to surmount all obstacles, Stanley pressed onward grimly. Having finally been shown a worthwhile objective, he had become obsessed with the need to achieve it. In his diary he wrote:

"Find him! Find him! Even the words are inspiring."

Though only five feet five inches tall, Stanley bore a determined expression that always made him seem taller. In Africa he found he had to develop patience and fortitude to accomplish even the simplest tasks. Just keeping his bearers and guards on their feet and moving was a nerve-racking ordeal. Shaw offered little help at rounding up defectors and keeping them moving, and the entire burden of responsibility fell on Stanley.

John Shaw, unfortunately, was a weak man. It soon became apparent that he had no interest in finding Livingstone. He cared only about his own comfort and pleasure.

The harassment Stanley had to endure from Tanganyika chiefs was equally exasperating. Each chief was willing to let the safari pass in peace only after Stanley assuaged his greed with gifts. This was called *honga* and meant a payment for trekking across the chief's land. Each tribe demanded an exorbitant amount of beads and cloth for its honga. Stanley had to bargain for hours with each.

Honga frequently presented itself in a curious form. When Stanley's horse died and he had his men bury it near the camp, the local chief came to discuss the matter in Swahili, the common East African language. Why had Stanley buried a horse on his land without asking permission? Now he would have to pay a honga of two doti—eight yards of cloth. Stanley, who was learning how to deal with African chiefs, remained calm.

"Are you the great chief of Kingaru?" he asked.
"Huh-uh. Yes."
"The great great chief?"
"Huh-uh. Yes."
"How many fighting men have you?"
"None."
"Oh! I thought you might have a thousand men with you, by your going to fine a strong white man, who has plenty of guns and soldiers, two doti for burying a dead horse."

The chief looked worried. He did not want to start a fight with the well-armed safari, but he still wanted his honga. He stubbornly maintained that Stanley had taken possession of his soil by using it for a burying ground without permission.

Needle in a Haystack

"I want no man's permission to do what is right," Stanley said. "My horse died. Had I left him to fester and stink in your valley, sickness would visit your village, your water would become unwholesome and caravans would not stop here for trade. But enough said. I understand you to say that you do not want him buried in your ground. The error I have fallen into is easily put right. This minute my soldiers shall dig him out again and cover up the soil as it was before and the horse shall be left where he died."

The bluff worked. The chief hastily said, "No, no, master! Let not the white man get angry. The horse is dead, and now lies buried. Let it remain so, since he is already there, and let us be friends again."

In June the safari entered the Unyanyembe territory where only three or four white men had been previously. The old caravan trail wandered almost aimlessly through dense jungled evergreens. Despite difficulties, the safari was making good time. On June 23 it reached Tabora.

Tabora was an Arab settlement some 500 miles west of Bagamoyo, and through its gateway passed the only known route to Ujiji. But Stanley had arrived at an inauspicious moment. A local war was brewing between the Arabs and a powerful bandit named Chief Mirambo who had been raiding villages in the area. Mirambo would not allow any caravans to use the Tabora-Ujiji route.

The Arabs had decided to vanquish Mirambo before

he ruined their trade. Stanley, determined to reach Ujiji—300 miles to the west—as quickly as possible, agreed to help them. Leaving the bulk of his safari behind, he and 50 guards marched out of Tabora with the Arabs.

The Arab force, slaves and soldiers, was over 2,000 strong. As the combined force approached Mirambo's stronghold, Stanley hoped the fighting would soon be over and he could resume his search for Livingstone. But events decided otherwise.

Just before the final assault against Mirambo, Stanley was knocked out of the fight by a burning fever. His men left him behind in a captured village and went off with the Arabs to the attack. Some time later young Selim burst into Stanley's hut and told him to flee for his life. Mirambo had defeated the Arabs and now was pursuing them. Four of Stanley's men had been killed in the battle and most of the others had fled.

Groggy with fever, Stanley stumbled from his hut to discover that the last of his panic-stricken men were on the verge of running and that John Shaw had every intention of going with them.

Stanley and the faithful Selim managed to stop seven and Shaw. When they reached a village near Tabora the next morning, Stanley began to plot a new course to Ujiji. Since a direct route to his goal was no longer available, he decided to make a detour south, thereby avoiding Mirambo's warriors.

To his dismay he found that only 13 of his Zanzibaris were willing to make the attempt with him. The rest were in such a panic to get away from Mirambo that they insisted on turning back. Stanley could not budge them. There was nothing he could do except to try to find new bearers. Shaw, as usual, was no help to him.

A few days later Stanley picked up a small Negro slave boy who said his name was Ndugu M'hali. He asked his bearers to find a more suitable name, and one suggested Kalulu, which meant young antelope in Swahili.

With a tin pan of water, Stanley christened the boy Kalulu and took him as his foster child.

On September 13 Stanley began his march to the south. He had managed to scrape together 54 men who said they would attempt to make the detour to Ujiji. The detour would take Stanley some 200 miles out of his way, but he had no alternative.

The next day 20 bearers deserted, and only nine could be found and brought back to the safari. Two others slipped off the following night. A few days later Shaw told Stanley he had a fever and was going back. He pleaded with Stanley to give up this madness of looking for a man who probably no longer existed, but Stanley was adamant. Shaw returned to Unyanyembe and died not long afterward.

Doggedly Stanley drove himself and his men on, striking south, then west, then north, into the uncharted territory of Western Tanganyika where no white man had been before. It was mostly savanna—broad undulating grasslands—where lions skulked and giraffes and zebras raced. The bearers began to mutter it would be a shame to leave this lush paradise which abounded in game.

Suddenly Stanley had a revolt on his hands.

Breaking camp one morning, he noticed that Asmani, the guide, and Bombay, the captain of the guards, started the trek in a sullen mood. Stanley and Selim stayed behind to prod on the stragglers. When they caught up with the safari a short time later, Stanley was surprised to see it had come to a halt. Loads had been dumped on the ground and the bearers were whispering in a huddle.

Stanley loaded his double-barreled shotgun and strolled toward the group without any sign of emotion. Seeing him come, the guards snatched up their rifles. Stanley continued to walk toward them, observing on his left the heads of Asmani and a guard lurking behind a large anthill. Both men were armed with muskets. Stanley raised his shotgun and called to them to come out.

With surly expressions the two men came from behind the anthill. The guard began to edge off to the right and Asmani's finger curved around the trigger of his musket. Stanley ordered him to lower his gun or he would shoot him, but the guide only moved closer with narrowed eyes. The guard was cautiously slipping around to get behind him when Stanley abruptly whirled about and rammed him in the chest with the

Needle in a Haystack

muzzle of his shotgun. The musket clattered to the ground as the guard fell and Stanley spun around again to confront Asmani.

In the instant when both men were ready to fire a loyal guard named Mabruki suddenly sprang forward and snatched Asmani's musket from him. The rebels, frightened and ashamed, promised to serve Stanley faithfully in the future.

In the next 28 days they made a hard trek through a bleak land where there was little game or water. On October 29 they tramped for 20 hours straight on one cup of tea per man. Then on the trunk of a lonely tree, Stanley carved a terse statement: *Starving. H.M.S.*

On November 1 they encountered a southbound caravan and the African in charge informed Stanley that a white man had recently arrived in Ujiji. Stanley was stunned. Could it possibly be Dr. Livingstone?

"How was he dressed?" he asked eagerly.

The same as Stanley the African replied.

"Is he young or old?"

"He is old. He has white hair on his face, and is sick."

"Where has he come from?"

"From a very far country away beyond Uguhha, called Manyuema."

"Indeed! And is he stopping at Ujiji now?"

"Yes, we saw him about eight days ago."

"Was he ever at Ujiji before?"

"Yes, he went away a long time ago."

Stanley was beside himself with delight. He was

The Man from Africa

certain it was Dr. Livingstone. No other white man was in Central Africa now except the famous missionary. Though still weakened by a recent attack of fever, he herded his little safari north with a renewed burst of energy, barely pausing for rest or food.

On November 2, only a day's march from Ujiji, Stanley rechalked his cork helmet, polished his best pair of boots, and donned a fresh suit. He had heard erroneous tales that Livingstone was something of a recluse who did not like other white men and he wanted to make himself as presentable as possible.

The next day was Friday, November 3, 1871, and the safari was only a few miles south of Ujiji. It had taken Stanley seven and a half months to reach this remote spot. He pushed on feverishly, fearful that Livingstone might already have left Ujiji for parts unknown.

The path plunged into a dense thorn thicket, zagged through tumbled rocks, and climbed a hill. It was a stiff climb that made Stanley sweat. Now and then he swung himself up with the help of low branches, and soon he left his bearers behind.

Eventually he gained a broad shelf of rock that jutted from the summit of the hill. There, below him, was vast and glittering Lake Tanganyika with Ujiji nestled on its nearest shore. From his lofty perch the village looked like a child's creation of mudpies.

Asmani took the lead with the American flag fluttering in the breeze, and the safari started down the hill. Tramping across a sundrenched savanna, Stanley told the guards to fire their guns into the air as they approached the village.

Almost at once two men clad in white ran out to see who was coming. Stanley told them his name, and they raced away. The Safari passed through a gate and across a compound. A great crowd of Negroes and Arabs shouldered up to gape at the strangers, and Stanley found himself walking down an avenue of mute people. He hoped his expression betrayed none of the emotion he felt.

A lone white man was standing, waiting, before the veranda of a low African bungalow. He was pale, wan, with gray whiskers and moustache. There was something about his tired face that reminded Stanley of his foster father: a certain look of wearied kindliness.

For a moment Stanley wanted to run to him and embrace him, but he was too shy to make such a public demonstration. Instead, he walked deliberately to the man, took off his helmet, and said the only thing he could think to say.

"Dr. Livingstone, I presume?"

"Yes," Livingstone said, smiling, lifting his cap.

The two men clasped hands, and Stanley let out his breath.

"I thank God, Doctor, I have been permitted to see you."

"I feel thankful that I am here to welcome you," Livingstone replied.

8. Stanley and Livingstone

THE ONLY two white men in Central Africa sat talking in the shade of Livingstone's veranda. Stanley quickly realized that Livingstone never for a moment had considered himself "lost" in Africa, as most of the world believed. He had been exactly where he wanted to be—in the Manyuema territory, searching for the true source of the White Nile.

It was something of a shock to Stanley. The man he had come so far to find had not been lost at all! This might change the complexion of his own position in Africa. It was one thing to rescue a desperate man from a wilderness; for such a man would be exceedingly grateful. But it was something else to try to rescue a man who didn't need or wish to be rescued; for such a man might easily become offended or downright indignant.

The Man from Africa

Stanley was uncertain how to bring up his reason for being there. Handing Livingstone a packet of letters from friends and relatives, which he had brought from Zanzibar, he said:

"I'm sure you must be impatient to read your letters after such a long silence."

Livingstone was actually in an agony to read news from home, but he was too polite to do such a thing in front of his newly arrived guest.

"I have waited years for letters," he said, "and can surely wait a few hours longer. I would rather hear the general news, so tell me how the world outside of Africa is getting along."

Stanley informed the doctor of the most recent and noteworthy events and then, attempting a shrewd approach to his problem, slipped into the subject of newspapers, asking, "You have heard of the New York *Herald*?"

"Oh yes," Livingstone replied, "who hasn't heard of that despicable newspaper?"

Despicable newspaper! How would Livingstone react when he learned that Stanley was a reporter sent by Bennett to find a sensational story for the "despicable" *Herald*? What if Livingstone became outraged and refused to give him a written document which he could take back to prove that he had actually found the doctor?

They passed the day talking in generalities. Incredible as it sounds, Stanley avoided any mention of his purpose in Tanganyika, and his well-mannered host did not question him about it. It was a rather strained meeting.

The next morning Stanley got up with the resolve that he would lay all his cards on the table. He found the doctor on the veranda and sat down with him. Then he got down to business.

"Doctor, you are probably wondering why I came here."

"I have been wondering. I thought at first that you were an emissary of the French Government—until I saw the American flag. To tell you the truth, I was rather glad it was so, because I could not have talked in French. And if you did not know English, we would have been a pretty pair of white men in Ujiji!"

Stanley laughed. "Well, for your sake I'm glad I am an American, and not a Frenchman, and that we can understand each other perfectly without an interpreter. . . . But, seriously, Doctor—now don't be startled when I tell you—I have come after *you*."

"After me!"

"Yes. Mr. James Gordon Bennett, son of the proprietor of the *Herald*, commissioned me to find you, to get what news of your discoveries you would like to give, and to assist you, if I can, with means."

"Young Mr. Bennett told you to come after me, to find me out and help me?" Livingstone was overwhelmed. "Well, indeed! I am very much obliged to him. And it makes me feel proud to think that you Americans think so much of me. You have just come in the proper time, for I was beginning to think that I should have to beg from the Arabs. Even they are in want of cloth, and there are but few beads in Ujiji. I wish I could embody my thanks to Mr. Bennett in suitable words."

Stanley was content. He and Livingstone were going to be good friends after all.

Stanley had very nearly missed Livingstone completely. The doctor had arrived at Ujiji less than two weeks ahead of him. Save for a stroke of chance, he would not have gone there at all, and Stanley would have had no way of learning his whereabouts.

Livingstone had discovered a mighty northbound river, which the Manyuemas called the Lualaba, and he had sensed that he was on the track of the source of the White Nile. Determined to follow the Lualaba to its mouth, he had traveled upriver to the village of Nyangwe where fever struck him and his supplies had dissipated. Ill and without the necessary means to go on, he had gone to Ujiji to seek help, though he had not actually expected to find any. He was so stunned by the timely and totally unexpected arrival of the Stanley-*Herald* expedition that he looked upon the young reporter as "the good Samaritan."

In the four months that Stanley spent with Livingstone, their somewhat reserved introduction to each other ripened into a close, personal relationship. Though exact opposites in many respects, there was a pronounced common bond between them. Both wanted to go where no man had been before, to see what no man had ever seen: to observe, record, locate and name it on a map.

Burton and Speke found Lake Tanganyika in 1858. They did not survey it; they simply looked at it, as if to say, "There it is," and went away. Speke found Victoria Nyanza (Lake Victoria) that same year; he did not survey it. Samuel Baker found Lake Albert in 1864, and did not survey it. All of these important landmarks were simply *discovered*, they were not explored. This was not Livingstone's way. He believed in painstaking exploration, and he taught Stanley to feel the same way.

Less than two weeks after their historic meeting the two men set out to explore the north tip of Lake Tanganyika. It was during this month-long voyage that Stanley became Livingstone's disciple: that is, he craved to carry out the work which he feared the aged doctor would not live to complete.

With the coming of the new year, Stanley realized he would have to start back to the coast. Livingstone's fragile health had not improved and Stanley wanted to take him home, but the doctor had no desire to leave Africa. He would stay there until he solved the riddle of the Lualaba. He did, however, go to Unyanyembe with the safari to collect the trade goods that Stanley had stored there for him. Stanley said he would send him more supplies once he had reached Zanzibar.

On March 14, 1872, the two friends said good-bye. It was a sad parting and a final one, both of them suspecting they would never see each other again. Then Stanley trekked into the east—into a long life of fame and disappointment. And Livingstone turned back to the west, to keep an appointment with his Maker on the lonely shore of Lake Bangweulu.

Stanley made a record journey to the coast without incident. No longer burdened with the extra supplies for Livingstone, his safari tramped from Tabora to Bagamoyo in 54 days, arriving there on May 6.

The Royal Geographical Society had recently sent a Livingstone Search and Relief expedition to Zanzibar and it was still in Bagamoyo when Stanley and his men arrived. The officers of this expedition were, to say the least, astounded when Stanley calmly informed them that they were too late, that he had already found Dr. Livingstone.

Stanley wanted them to continue with their expedition, pointing out that Livingstone was alone and ill and needed all the help and supplies he could get. Mirambo was still on the rampage in the interior and Stanley knew that Livingstone would have trouble finding loyal bearers. And here was a ready-made expedition that could be put at his disposal.

The officers talked over the matter and decided there was no reason for them to go on. They would dissolve the expedition and return home. The truth probably was that they were irked because Stanley, a mere reporter, an American nobody, had managed to do what the British Government and the Royal Geographical Society had twice failed to do.

Stanley left them in disgust and crossed over to Zanzibar. There he hired 54 men and started them on their way with more supplies for his friend—the man who was willing to die to solve a geographical problem.

The historic expedition was over. In 13 and one half months Stanley had trekked 2,250 miles—two-thirds of it through totally unexplored territory. The search for Livingstone had cost the lives of 20 men, white and black, and disease had reduced Stanley's stocky frame to a mere 90 pounds.

No matter, the job had been done. He had not only found the story of the century—he had also found one of its greatest men.

He sailed from Zanzibar at the end of May, not knowing he was entering one of the darkest periods of his life.

9. Hero's Return

ARRIVING in France in the summer of 1872, Stanley found himself honored and sought after in a manner that left him astonished. He had expected to be recognized for having found Livingstone, but he had not anticipated such an overwhelming ovation.

Reporters, publishers, royalty, explorers, historians, social-climbers and various organizations pursued him night and day with questions, invitations, arguments. He tried to satisfy them as best he could, but it was impossible. Bennett, disturbed because he felt that Stanley's story was the exclusive property of the *Herald*, fired a two-word cable at him: "Stop talking."

But he couldn't. People hounded him even into his hotel room. Meanwhile, in England, a bitter controversy was growing.

Stanley had unwittingly put the noses of a great many Britons out of joint. Who was this unknown

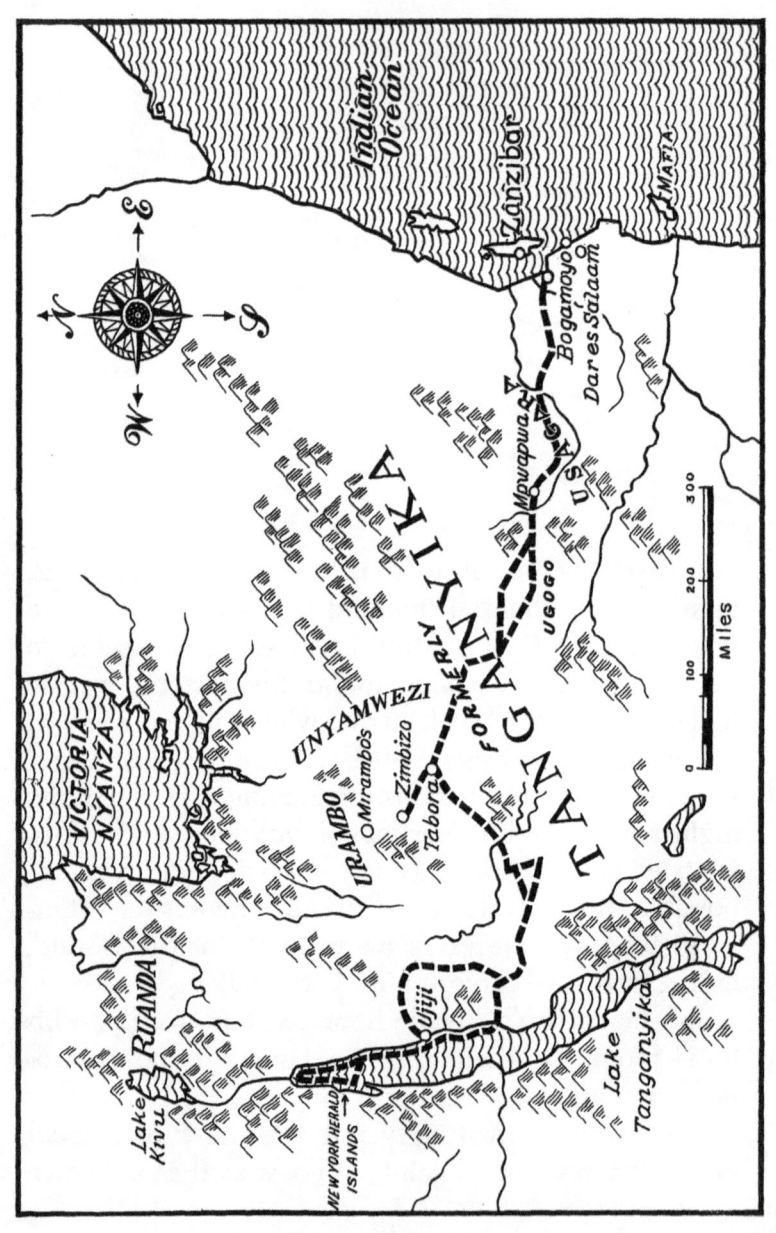

Route of Stanley's Search for Livingstone

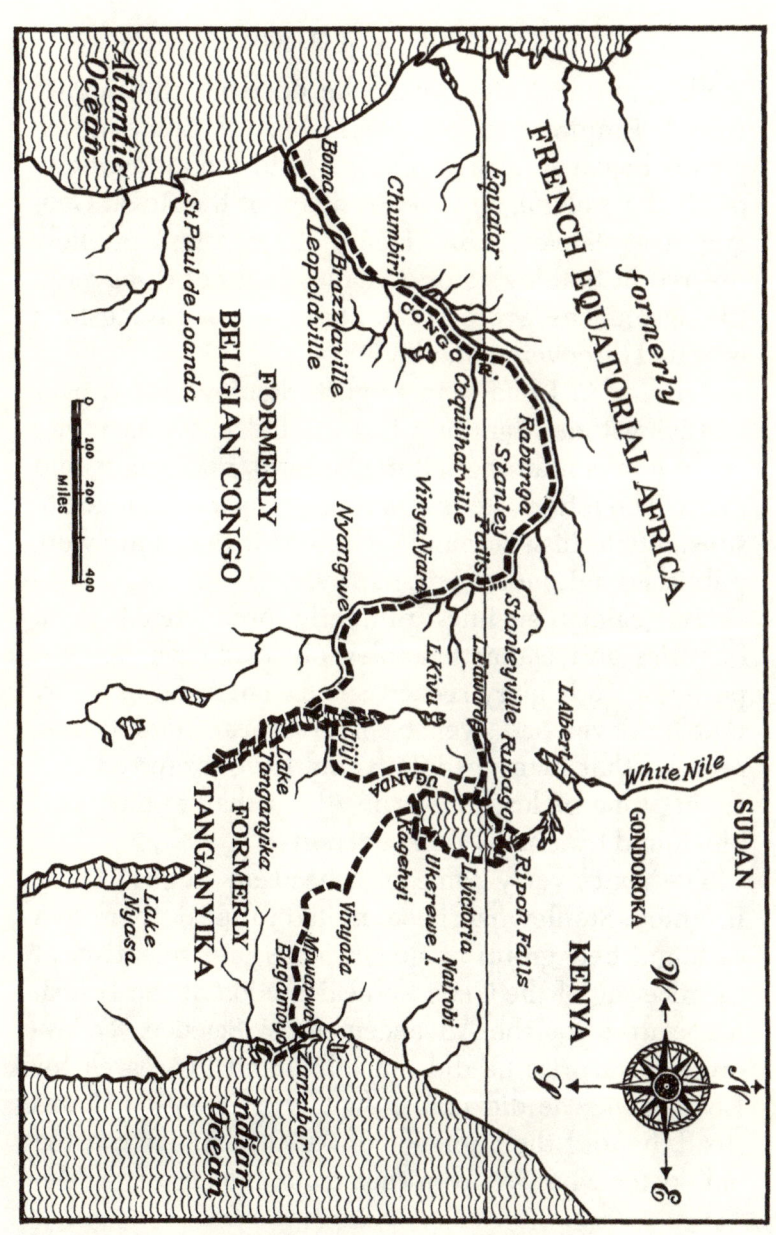

Stanley's Route across Africa

Yankee upstart? How could he do what the mighty British Empire had not been able to? Some newspapers began to express doubts as to the authenticity of Stanley's claim, and the President of the Royal Geographical Society, Sir Henry Rawlinson, publicly sneered at Stanley's story. Stanley had not discovered Livingstone, he wrote to the *Times,* it was Livingstone who had discovered Stanley!

Arriving in London in August, Stanley turned over to Livingstone's family a box the old missionary had given him containing letters, journals, documents and maps. The letters, he felt, were competent evidence to substantiate his story and he saw to it that some were published in London newspapers.

His jealous enemies promptly pronounced them forgeries and claimed Stanley obviously was an imposter, a crude glory-seeker. Some went as far as to say that he never had even been to Africa. Stanley soon realized that many people would have preferred that Livingstone be lost forever in Africa than to have had him found by a mere Yankee reporter.

The controversy came to a head on August 15, at Brighton. Stanley had been invited to speak there to a distinguished group of geographers and scientists at the meeting of the Geographical Section of the British Association for the Advancement of Science. To everyone's surprise he did not talk about his search for Livingstone; he did not, in fact, even mention it. Instead, he told the audience of 3,000 people about the old doctor who was even then tramping across the African wilderness to discover the sources of the Nile. He related to them the vogage he and Livingstone had made on the northern end of Lake Tanganyika, and then concluded his talk.

The learned members were not satisfied. Some acid comments were directed at Stanley, and the chairman stated they had not come there to listen to sensational stories. They wanted *serious facts*. They began to question him, to challenge his every statement. Several made a pointed attack on Livingstone's theory regarding the Lualaba River, and one scholarly gentleman even suggested that Dr. Livingstone's mind was "wandering."

It was apparent to Stanley that he had not been invited to the meeting merely as a speaker. He was being called upon to defend himself, as if he were in a court of law charged with a crime. He had always been cursed with a short temper, and now he replied with barely repressed fury. In his opinion, he told them, Livingstone was right about the Lualaba. But, right or wrong, they should have the decency to treat the doctor's theory with respect. He went on to imply that they were only "armchair geographers" who told one another theories about the Nile, while Livingstone had spent half of his life seeking out the truth.

He stalked out of the meeting an embittered man.

Within a few days Livingstone's family announced that the documents Stanley had brought from Africa were genuine. Those who had so viciously criticized him found themselves in a state of embarrassment.

The Man from Africa

There could no longer exist any question of forgery. The Geographical Society reversed its opinion and gave Stanley a vote of thanks. He was awarded a diamond-studded gold snuffbox from Queen Victoria "in recognition of the prudence and zeal displayed by him in opening communication with Doctor Livingstone, and thus relieving the general anxiety felt in regard to the fate of that distinguished traveller."

But the damage to Stanley's touchy pride and his sense of fair play had already been done, and he was in no mood for belated thanks. He sailed on a steamer bound for New York. He had not seen his adopted land for five long years.

America was ready and willing to receive its famous adopted son. He was feted at the pier and a celebration party was given for him at the *Herald* building. Oddly enough, James Gordon Bennett, Jr., did not attend this happy function. Stanley saw Bennett later in the day and they had a rather strained meeting which lasted only a few minutes.

Apparently Bennett was displeased with his illustrious reporter, perhaps even jealous. To his mind, Stanley's story was supposed to have belonged exclusively to the *Herald*. But Stanley's sudden fame was putting the newspaper in the shade. After all, Stanley had been a nobody before Bennett hired him; it had been Bennett's idea to find Livingstone, it had been Bennett's money that footed the expense. And now Stanley was walking off with all the glory.

Hero's Return

Bennett was never able to forgive Stanley. Later in life he was known to make derogatory remarks about his employee. Stanley, on the other hand, never said a word against Bennett, verbally or in print.

But if Bennett had received him coldly, it was not so with the American public. Stanley quickly found himself involved in a series of tours, lectures, banquets and receptions. He had written a book, *How I Found Livingstone in Central Africa*, which was published in November 1872, and it quickly became a best-seller. He was not as fortunate in his public lectures, however.

First, there was the problem of his untutored voice; one can easily imagine him speaking in a strange mixture of Welsh mumble, Southern drawl, Yankee twang, and African singsong. Secondly, he lost his audience's interest by telling them of Livingstone's efforts and tribulations rather than describing his own experiences in finding him. And he was shy, embarrassed, lacking in self-composure. In short, he suffered acutely from stage fright.

The newspapers deplored his elocution in their reviews—and this included his own paper, the New York *Herald*! Stanley gave up public speaking after his third lecture.

Aside from this minor setback, he was still enjoying fame. Florence Nightingale, the famous English nurse, compared Stanley's achievement with the story of Humpty-Dumpty—that is to say that all the "Queen's men" (meaning the British Government and all its societies) could not set Livingstone up again. It took a Stanley to do it.

And America's most famous humorist, Mark Twain, said:

"I am not here to disparage Columbus . . . but when you come to regard the achievements of these two men, Columbus and Stanley, from the standpoint of the difficulties they encountered, the advantage is with Stanley and against Columbus. Now, Columbus started out to discover America. Well, he didn't need to do anything at all but sit in the cabin of his ship and hold his grip and sail straight on, and America would discover itself. Here it was, barring his passage the whole length and breadth of the South American continent, and he couldn't get by it. He'd got to discover it. But Stanley started out to find Doctor Livingstone, who was scattered abroad, as you might say, over the length and breadth of a vast slab of Africa as big as the United States."

By the first of the year there were three plays on Broadway about Stanley and Livingstone, and even street urchins were tipping their ragged caps and saying, "Dr. Livingstone, I presume?"

Stanley began to suspect that these few words he had uttered in Africa—simply because they had seemed to be the most appropriate for the occasion—were destined to outlive him. But he could not understand why everyone took such delight in repeating them.

Then his past began to catch up with him.

Hero's Return

Suddenly all of America wanted to know who this man was. Who were his parents? Where was he born, and what had he been before he went to Africa to find Livingstone? An abundance of theories, rumors, accusations, and eyewitness stories quickly began to circulate in answer to these probing questions. Various theories named Stanley as being everything from a descendant of the royal Polish family to a native backwoodsman of Missouri. The most damaging story came from Louis Noe, who leveled various charges and lies against his old friend.

His past was the one thing Stanley did not want explored. It would not help his or Livingstone's cause to have the world discover that he was a runaway from a workhouse, a ship-jumper, a turncoat in the Civil War, and a deserter from the U.S. Navy. It puzzled him that so many people wanted to attack his personal character when he had never intentionally harmed any living man.

He had discovered that fame could be too much of a burden for one man to carry in his lifetime. The idolization, the criticism, the lionization, the slander, the gaudy tinsel, the acid abuse, and the persistent prying into his personal life were more than he was ready to cope with. He would much rather have faced a wilderness filled with wild animals and savage warriors.

After finishing his second book, a juvenile tale called *My Kalulu* (Kalulu himself was at that time attending a boarding school in England), Stanley made his decision. He wanted to be free and independent again, to see new places, observe stirring events—to accomplish something! Bennett was back in Paris, and on May 2, 1873, Stanley arrived there to ask for a new assignment.

Bennett handed him the new Carlist war in Spain, and Stanley departed in an elated mood. Neither he nor the rest of the world knew it at the time, but Livingstone had died only 24 hours before in a nameless region that would one day become Zambia.

After several violent outbursts of fighting, the Carlists were hemmed in along the north coast of Spain and the revolt fizzled into guerrilla warfare. Stanley impatiently began to cast about for something new. Hearing that England was sending a military force to West Africa to fight the Ashanti savages on the Gold Coast, he eagerly seized the opportunity to return to Africa—that dark, brooding, mysterious land with which he had become so strangely infatuated.

Arriving at Cape Coast Castle on the Ashanti coast, he learned that General Wolseley's expeditionary force was bogged down by a lack of supplies and reinforcements. Stanley had to sit with the idle troops and do the one thing he hated most: wait.

The Ashantis were led by a brutal chieftain called King Coffee (Kofi Karikari). They had been systematically raiding the villages of a peaceful tribe known as the Fantees, who were under the protective wing of the British colonial system. For the preceding 50 years the Ashantis had been conducting fearful massacres in the interior, had annihilated a small British force, and routed another. According to popular fancy, King Coffee used a defeated British general's skull for a drinking cup. Thus the British were eager to launch a punitive expedition against Coomassie, the capital of the Ashantis.

But they were not eager enough for Stanley's restless nature. Learning that a Captain Glover had already proceeded into the interior to engage the enemy with a handful of troops, Stanley left the army and went up the Volta River to join the aggressive captain. Still, there was little action. Stanley was merely a spectator.

Reinforcements arrived on the Gold Coast just before Christmas. By January 6, 1874, Wolseley had his army on the march for Coomassie. King Coffee's stronghold was surrounded by a vast jungle filled with malarial swamps which the army had to cross. All paths to and from the abandoned Ashanti villages had been lined with human sacrifices, the severed heads of the victims pegging the track like milestones.

The army tramped and waded through this land of horror for more than three arduous weeks. Then, on January 31, it met the Ashantis in full force at Amoaful and fought a decisive battle. Stanley and the other journalists had been instructed to remain with the rear guard for their own protection, but he and war correspondent Winwood Reid went forward with the front fighting line. Following rapidly in the wake of the battle, they had to pass through clumps of dead, dying and wounded men. Soon they found themselves in the hottest sector of the fighting.

There was nothing for them to do but snatch up rifles and bandoleers and fight for their lives. As newspaper correspondents they were supposed to be noncombatants, but that was something the screaming Ashanti warriors could not be expected to know. Dropping to a kneeling position to steady his aim, Stanley hastily opened fire on the flood of painted savages sweeping toward the British line. General Wolseley happened to notice Stanley during the fighting and later stated that "he looked as cool and self-possessed as if he had been at target practice."

Coomassie fell on February 5 and the British burned it to the ground. The Ashanti campaign was over, and Stanley was glad. He was 33 now and war no longer seemed a grand adventure. Adventure was pitting yourself against the forces of nature, seeking out the world's multitude of mysteries, uncovering the answers to the secrets that had puzzled man for thousands of years. He discovered that he was even tiring of journalism; playing the part of the romantic war correspondent had lost its enchantment.

He was about to return to England when he learned of Dr. Livingstone's death. The doctor's lifelong mission in Africa should not be brought to a halt by his death. Someone else would have to go forward and complete the work. And Stanley looked upon himself as Livingstone's heir. He felt that the legacy of Africa had been left in his hands.

10. The Way to Lualaba

DR. LIVINGSTONE'S BODY—preserved in salt by his faithful African followers—reached England on April 15, 1874, nearly a year after his death. Stanley served as one of the pallbearers, helping to lay the body of his old friend to rest in Westminster Abbey. Then he turned to the matter at hand: Livingstone's legacy.

Many of Africa's geographical mysteries remained unsolved. Stanley felt he was the man to solve them. His decision made, he went to the *Daily Telegraph* newspaper in London and presented his plan to the editor. Briefly, he intended to circumnavigate Lakes Victoria and Tanganyika and solve the mystery of the Lualaba River. Would the *Daily Telegraph* give him backing?

The editor approved of the project but wondered if

Stanley was capable of completing such a monumental undertaking. Stanley's answer was quite candid. Africa offered so many dangers from man, beast and climate that he did not know if he would live long enough to be successful. But he would certainly do his best to make a systematic exploration of all the regions he had named.

This satisfied the editor and he said he would go along with the proposal if Bennett would agree to split the expense. They cabled the New York *Herald* and received Bennett's characteristic reply that same day: "Yes."

Stanley led a safari of 356 men out of Bagamoyo on November 16, 1874, and struck northwest for Victoria Nyanza. With him went three ill-fated white men: a young hotel clerk, Fred Barker, and brothers named Frank and Edward Pocock. Stanley's adopted son Kalulu was also a member of the expedition.

This time Stanley traveled as an experienced explorer with a bigger and better equipped safari. Nevertheless, disaster dogged his trail night and day. There were dysentery, fever and desertions. Again the heat reached 128 degrees. Three men died of heat exhaustion in December; Edward Pocock died of typhus in January; the guides deserted; the food ran out and the safari had to live off the land. By the end of the first two months there had been 20 deaths and 89 desertions.

Open hostility greeted the weakened caravan as it

The Way to Lualaba

entered the Ituri territory. Warriors lurking in the bush began to pick off stragglers. One bearer who fell behind was dismembered. The Zanzibaris cried out for revenge, wanting to sack and burn the local villages, but Stanley refused.

"Revenge," he told them, "what good will that do? You talk of my giving a lesson to these people. I did not come to Africa to give such lessons."

But he was forced to give in the next day as hordes of warriors started to press the column's flanks, growing bolder as they drummed up courage for a mass attack. Suddenly they surged forward in a howling wave, and the three white men and the guards were hard pressed to hold them back with rapid rifle fire.

Stanley, seeing a village in the distance, ordered his men to attack and burn it. This fire helped to distract the warriors, and the safari managed to escape into the forest, leaving behind 22 dead. It took two weeks to fight their way clear of Ituri. By then the safari was down to 212 men.

They made friends with the people of Mombiti, where Stanley purchased food and hired fresh bearers, and on February 27 they reached the shores of Victoria Nyanza. Leaving the bulk of the expedition at the village of Kagehyi, Stanley embarked on the lake with ten men in a 40-foot cedar boat named *Lady Alice*.

The first two months went well. By careful measurements and calculations Stanley was able to establish that Victoria was the largest lake in Africa and the second largest freshwater lake in the world. Then, one day when they were about to land in a wooded cove to search for food, they heard a spine-tingling war cry: *"Hehu-ah hehu-uuu!"*

"Cast off quickly!" Stanley cried. "Backwater on the oars!"

Too late! A gang of spear- and club-wielding warriors poured from the underbrush, ran through the shallows, and seized the boat's gunwales. In a moment they had raised the boat and its stunned crew from the water and were rushing it 20 yards up the pebbly shore! Dumping the boat on the shore, some 200 shouting and gesticulating savages pressed around Stanley and his men with flashing spears.

Stanley started to reach for his pistols, but changed his mind when he realized the utter hopelessness of their situation. With a dozen spears poised only a few feet from his head, he remained sitting with a calm expression. It worked. The savages were puzzled by this remarkable lack of emotion. Their frenzy simmered down and they grudgingly pulled back from the stranded boat and began to mutter to one another, wondering what they should do next. Stanley spoke to his men in a low voice.

"Do you think you can push this boat into the water . . . with all her goods in her, before those men can reach us?"

They said they could.

"Stand by, then. Range yourselves on both sides of the boat, carelessly." Turning to one, he said, "Safeni,

The Way to Lualaba

take these cloths on your arm, walk up toward the men on the hill. Open out the cloths one by one, as though you were admiring the pattern. When I call out to you, throw the cloths away and fly to us."

Safeni walked over to the savages with the cloth, pretending he wanted to barter with them. Stanley's men were now leaning against the gunwales, and he spoke to them in a whisper.

"Ready, boys? Lay hold firmly. Break the boat rather than stop. It's life or death." He looked around. Safeni was displaying his colorful cloth to the warriors.

"Push!" Stanley said. "Push, Saramba, Kirango, Baraka!"

The Zanzibaris heaved with all their strength, driving the heavy boat stern-first across the pebbles. One of the savages saw the maneuver and cried a warning. In the next instant the warriors came yelling down the shore.

"Safeni!" Stanley roared, swinging up his Winchester repeater. The lunging boat was nearing the water. Safeni was racing toward it. The *Lady Alice* splashed into the shallows and glided out, carrying the clinging Zanzibaris along with her.

"Swim away with her!" Stanley cried. "Don't stop!"

A savage with a raised spear was leaping behind Safeni. Stanley shot him with his Winchester, and Safeni took a wild dive into the water as Stanley continued to pump slugs into the raging warriors. By now the crew was piling into the boat and reaching for their rifles. Stanley dropped the empty Winchester, snatched up his shotgun, and fired both barrels. The bedraggled and heroic Safeni was hauled into the boat as the *Lady Alice* got away in a rain of arrows and spears.

The boat returned to Kagehyi late in May. Frank Pocock, Kalulu and the Zanzibaris greeted the voyagers with a cheer. But someone was missing.

"Where is Fred Barker?" Stanley asked.

"He died 12 days ago of a fever, and lies there." Frank pointed to a fresh grave near the shore.

Stanley and Pocock were now the only two white men in a vast region of equatorial Africa.

Stanley had wanted to go north to Lake Albert, but the way was blocked by a war between the Waganda and the Wavuma tribes. The Waganda were friendly to Stanley and assured him that the war would soon be over. But they were wrong. At the end of ten weeks it was still going strong, and Stanley resolved to settle it himself.

The Wavuma stronghold on an island in Lake Victoria appeared to be impregnable. So Stanley lashed together three big war canoes, erected a tall wooden tower on them, and decorated it with plumes, fronds and flags. He then sent a messenger to the island to proclaim that a terrible monster filled with powerful magic was coming to devastate the Wavumas. That night the Wagandas paddled the weird-looking dread-

The Way to Lualaba

nought close to the island, and a man on top of the tower called to the enemy in a sepulchral voice.

"Speak! What will you do? Will you make peace with us, or shall we blow up your island? Be quick and answer!"

The Wavumas' answer was prompt. They would make peace!

The way north was now open, but because of untrustworthy guides Stanley did not reach Lake Albert. He did, however, locate Lake Edward some 150 miles west of Victoria Nyanza, but a new tribal conflict prevented him from exploring it. Early in 1876 he turned south and proceeded to Ujiji, arriving on March 27. It had been exactly four years since he had last left this now historic site.

He immediately began the circumnavigation of Lake Tanganyika, a project that lasted a little over seven weeks and that positively established it as the world's longest freshwater lake. He also found that it had only one outlet, the Lukuga River which streamed westward to feed the mysterious Lualaba.

With Lake Victoria and Lake Tanganyika behind him he was now ready for the final tremendous task, the one for which Livingstone had given his life—to trace the course of the Lualaba River and to settle once and for all whether it was the source of the Congo or the Niger or the Nile. Even Livingstone had had doubts about the Lualaba, fearing that it might turn out to be the Congo. He had been willing to die to prove it was the Nile, but he had wondered who would risk being cooked in a cannibal pot to find that it was only the Congo River?

Stanley would risk it. He could not have peace of mind until he had completed the legacy his best friend had left him. Still beset with desertions, he managed to push his safari to Nyangwe on the Lualaba by late October.

The territory that contained the Lualaba was not called the Belgian Congo in 1876. It was indicated on maps of Africa with the dubious words UNKNOWN TERRITORY. But certain grim things were known about it, at least by hearsay. The Arab slave traders said that to the north and west the Lualaba ran through a frightful country of cannibals, pythons, leopards and gorillas.

These tales demoralized Stanley's men so completely that he had grave doubts as to whether they would actually follow him down the fearsome Lualaba. He and Frank Pocock discussed the problem from every aspect. Should they follow this great river that had been flowing mysteriously north for thousands of years? Or should they swing across to Uganda and make their way back to Zanzibar?

"Let's toss a coin," Frank suggested. "Best two out of three to decide it."

"Toss away, Frank. Heads for the north and the Lualaba; tails for the south."

They tossed a rupee—and it landed tails six times in a row. Fate appeared doing its best to steer them away

The Way to Lualaba

from the Lualaba, but Stanley chose to ignore the omen.

"It's no use, Frank. We'll face our destiny, despite the rupee. With your help, I'll follow the river."

"Have no fear of me," Frank responded. "I'll stand by you."

Realizing that he would need a strong armed escort to get his safari down the Lualaba, Stanley went to an Arab called Tippu-Tib—the most renowned slave and ivory trader in equatorial Africa. Tippu-Tib liked Stanley, but he could not understand his motives.

"If you white people are fools enough to throw away your lives, that is no reason why Arabs should. What is this river to you? What do you want to know about it?"

Stanley tried to explain that civilization had advanced by learning. "Otherwise, mankind would dwell in darkness forever."

Tippu-Tib shrugged and called to an Arab who had once ventured north of Nyangwe. "Speak, Abed. Tell us what you know of this river."

"I know all about the river, praise be to Allah!"

"In what direction does it flow?"

"It flows north."

"And then?"

"Still north. I tell you, sir, it flows north, and north, and north, and there is no end to it. I think it reaches the Salt Sea."

"Well, point out the direction in which this Salt Sea is."

"God only knows."

Tippu-Tib looked at Stanley as if to say, "You see?" And Stanley then got down to the heart of the matter. He offered the equivalent of 5,000 dollars for an escort —which was reason enough for Tippu-Tib to go anywhere! The wily old Arab said he would join the safari along with 700 of his followers.

It was a great relief to Stanley. His own 200 men were so frightened by the prospect of penetrating the cannibal country that they were on the brink of mutiny. But in a 900-man expedition they could march with confidence.

Stanley started down the Lualaba on November 5, 1876.

11. Cannibal Country

AT FIRST they trekked across a vast savanna where the grass grew waist-deep and a thin pallor of heat haze lay. Then they swung into the almost impenetrable tangle of the Mitumba forest.

Hacking their way through the primeval forest, over giant fallen trees that barricaded the way, they averaged only six miles a day in the first week. Everyone but Stanley was demoralized by this brutal land.

When it became impossible to transport the *Lady Alice* through the jungle, Stanley and his crew started to boat down the river while Tippu-Tib followed with the rest of the expedition on land.

Thus far they had not been met with hostility. They saw many villages, but all were empty. Stanley would not let his men loot the huts, as he wanted it known that he had come in peace. But, unfortunately, peace was not what the local Africans had in mind. The safari was attacked time and again in the next two weeks, by disease as well as savages. Twelve men died of smallpox and were buried in the river.

The painful, nervous struggle down the mysterious river by land and water dragged on. War cries wailed from the jungle and poison-tipped reed arrows winged at the expedition.

On December 18 there was a concerted attack in an effort to annihilate the safari. Stanley, on shore directing the fighting, led his party in a hasty retreat to a mud village on the river bank. The isolated huddle of huts was the center of countless faint paths that came to it from all directions. It was surrounded by a thorn *boma* (a rough stockade).

After capturing the village, Stanley manned the stockade with his entire force. The attackers pulled back into the bush and began to snipe with arrows, maintaining their harassment throughout the night. The next dawn Stanley was appalled to see a great flotilla of war canoes racing toward the besieged village. Nearly 800 painted and plumed savages were descending upon his position. Piling ashore, they threw themselves at the thorn barricade.

Throughout the day the warriors attacked in frenzied waves, only to be repulsed by the furious fire of Snider rifles. At nightfall they withdrew to an island in the river. Stanley, knowing they would renew the attack in the morning, decided to outfox them.

In the darkness he and his crew slipped across the

river in the *Lady Alice* and around the island to the spot where the savages had moored their 38 canoes. Cutting the canoes loose, the Zanzibaris quietly herded them down the river to a point where Frank Pocock and some men received them. One by one the huge craft were hauled into the fortified village. Then they waited to see what the savages would do in the morning.

There was little the savages could do when they awoke and found themselves stranded on the island. Stanley went out and had a peace conference with them, and they soon came to terms: No more war, and they would sell him 23 of the canoes he had captured.

Thus ended the first war with the savages, but not the war with disease. Smallpox was still landing deadly blows on the safari, and Tippu-Tib finally reached the end of his endurance. He told Stanley he was going to return to Nyangwe with his men. It would take a drastic toll in Stanley's force. But at least he could now put all of his people on the river in canoes. Yet would they follow him without Tippu-Tib's support?

"Into whichever sea this great river empties, there shall we follow it," he said to his uneasy men. "You have seen that I have saved you a score of times when everything looked black and dismal for us.... All I ask of you is perfect trust in whatever I say. On your lives depends my own; if I risk yours, I risk mine.... Sons of Zanzibar, lift up your heads and be men. What is

THE MAN FROM AFRICA

there to fear? Here we are all together, like one family with hearts united. . . . Strike your paddles deep, and cry 'Bismillah,' and let us go forward."

The Zanzibaris were understandably apprehensive. Yet they had a deep-rooted trust in this strange white man who never recognized fear. They shouted *"Bismillah!"* (in the name of God) and followed him down the river. It was New Year's, 1877.

Passing through the Vinya-Njara country they encountered enemies on nearly every mile of river bank. The painted savages came streaming out of the villages and into war canoes, crying, "Meat! Meat!" Again and again the safari fleet and the cannibal canoes held vicious engagements on the roiling river.

Soon they came to one of nature's obstacles: cataracts—50 miles of treacherous rapids. It was dangerous work piloting the 23 canoes through the swift, broken current and around the multitudes of snaggle-toothed rocks. Canoes were swamped, supplies were lost, men had to be rescued. One canoe was pounded to matchwood at the foot of a swirling fall. In many places the cataracts were too wild to be navigated, and the men had to hack paths through the jungle and carry their canoes and supplies.

It took one month of fighting rapids, jungle, savages and red ants to pass around this formidable barricade. As soon as the safari took to the water again they were attacked by a large army of Wane-Mpungu—cannibals who filed their teeth and tattooed their faces. But

Stanley had become adept at jungle fighting and he defeated the Wane-Mpungu and captured many of their warriors.

After getting around the rapids they camped on the site of what would become Stanleyville (and today is called Kisangani in the Republic of the Congo). Now the mysterious river was a mile wide and had a distinct westward trend. There could be little doubt as to what it indicated. Livingstone had been wrong. Neither the Nile nor the Niger, the Lualaba was actually a headstream of the great Congo River which emptied into the Atlantic Ocean.

War drums throbbed along the shore, war horns moaned in the jungle, war cries rang across the river as the *Lady Alice* led the 22 canoes down the mighty Congo.

On February 1, 1877, they fought their biggest river battle. Reaching the mouth of the Aruwimi River at noon, Stanley saw 54 enormous war canoes poised for an attack.

He hastily ordered his canoes into a long battle line and jockeyed the *Lady Alice* in front of his line. The flotilla raced upon them, a huge war canoe leading the way. There were 80 paddlers in the lead craft, their naked bodies bending in unison as they chanted and plied their paddles. Standing in the bow were ten parrot-plumed warriors waving spears. The crashing sound of drums, the blaring of ivory horns, and a scalp-tingling chorus from 2,000 savage throats threw Stanley's little force into a state of near panic.

"Be firm as iron!" he called to his men. "Wait until you see the first spear, and then take good aim. . . . Don't think of running away, for only your guns can save you."

Suddenly the huge war canoe drove straight for the *Lady Alice* as if it meant to ram her. At the last tense moment it veered off to present its broadside and fired a flight of arrows and spears. The safari flotilla opened up with Sniders and dozens of gaudy savages toppled into the churning water.

The enemy fleet drew back up the river to reorganize itself, and Stanley instantly took the initiative, ordering his battle line forward. As the little safari flotilla drove up the river in battle order, the cannibals lost heart and tried to retreat. Stanley kept after them, however, driving them aground on mud banks with rifle fire.

Piling ashore, the yelling Zanzibaris chased the demoralized cannibals deep into the jungle. Arriving at a village, they quickly captured it and looted its ivory tusks. Wandering around the village, Stanley saw the grisly evidence: Among the ashes of the cookfires were empty skulls, scorched ribs and a half-eaten human forearm. Sickened by this barbaric sight, he recalled his men to the river.

Now 400 miles and 88 days away from Nyangwe, they had fought 28 battles. Seventy-nine safari members were already dead. Though they did not know it, they still had more than 1,300 miles to go before the river reached the sea.

Stanley, determined as ever to go on, began to harbor secret misgivings about the outcome of his rash venture. Livingstone had said that floating down the Lualaba might prove to be a foolhardy feat, and Stanley was beginning to think it was true. As he made his notes in his journal he couldn't help but feel that they would never be read by any man.

On down the dark and deadly river the safari proceeded: fighting, surveying, starving, trading, struggling with nature. By mid-February they were in the Rubunga and Urangi country, and on February 14 they were skirting the village of the Bangala. This tribe was ferocious and well organized; worse, they had somehow acquired ancient Portuguese muskets. They came rushing from their village yelling a war cry.

Stanley stood up in the *Lady Alice* and called, "Sennenneh!" (Peace!) The Bangala did not respond. They began to fan out in their war canoes, eyeing the safari hungrily. Frank Pocock started to aim his rifle, but Stanley ordered him to put it down. He tried to barter with the savages, offering them his trade goods. But the Bangalas had something else in mind. They could not *eat* beads or cloth.

Without warning, they discharged a musket broadside into Stanley's boat, wounding three of his crew. The Zanzibaris promptly replied with their rapid-firing Sniders and the Bangala retreated in disorder.

The Man from Africa

Stanley, still standing squarely in the bow of his boat, a perfect target for any savage, calmly led his canoes past the hostile shore. It was the thirty-second battle—and the last. Stanley had been in the midst of every fight and not received a scratch. He attributed this, in part, to the color of his skin. The savages had never seen a white man before, and his strange aspect bewildered them.

"Had I been a black man, I should long before have been slain," he later said. "But even in the midst of a battle, curiosity stronger than hate or bloodthirstiness arrested the sinewy arm which drew the bow, and delayed the flying spear."

On March 12 they entered a lakelike expansion of the Congo River which was about 80 square miles in area. Frank named it Stanley Pool. (On its southern shore today stands the capital of the Republic of the Congo, Kinshasa, formerly called Léopoldville.) They then encountered a chain of rapids that consisted of 32 cataracts, which Stanley named Livingstone Falls. (Later it was renamed Stanley Falls.)

It was impossible to ride down these roaring cataracts. No man ever has. In working around the wild water, one man broke his back, another his head, and Stanley once plunged into a 30-foot crevice but escaped with slight cuts. One canoe bearing eight persons, including Stanley's foster son Kalulu, was sucked over the highest falls and all perished.

Sadly, Stanley named the spot Kalulu Falls.

Though they had no way of knowing it, they were

only about 200 miles from the Atlantic coast. Still disaster continued to haunt them in the swift water. Canoes were smashed to splinters, 50 ivory tusks were lost overboard, trade goods and general cargo sank out of sight forever. Stanley was nearly swept into a watery grave when the *Lady Alice* went out of control and barely missed being sucked into a great whirlpool. In his words:

"Never did the rocks assume such hardness, such solemn grimness and bigness, never were they invested with such terrors and such grandeur of height, as while we were the cruel sport and prey of the brown-black waves, which whirled us around like a spinning top, swung us aside, almost engulfed us in the rapidly subsiding troughs, and then hurled us upon the white rageful crests of others."

Late in April they had to make a two-week portage over a mountain in order to bypass the mighty Inkisi Falls, which the local inhabitants said were the last of the waterfalls. Stanley made camp in Mowa and gave his men a well-earned rest. A few days later the Mowas, who had been friendly, suddenly descended upon his camp waving muskets and spears and howling war cries.

When Stanley asked what was wrong, they said they had seen him writing in a book, which they called a *tara-tara*. They feared it was black magic that would harm their land.

"Our country will waste, our goats will die, our bananas will rot," they said. "We have gathered together to fight you if you do not burn that tara-tara now.... If you burn it, we go away."

The book they referred to was Stanley's notebook containing most of his geographical data. He would as soon have given away his right hand as destroy his precious notes. Going to his tent, he dug out his dog-eared copy of Shakespeare, which was the same shape and color as his notebook, and took it to the Mowas.

"Is this the tara-tara that you wish burned?"

"Yes, yes, that is it! We will not touch it. It is fetish. You must burn it."

"Well, let it be so," Stanley said. "I will do anything to please my good friends of Mowa."

He took the book to the nearest fire and tossed it into the flames. The Mowas watched Shakespeare burn with sighs of relief and went away satisfied.

On June 3, after a full week of rest, the safari was prepared to shoot the Massassa and Zinga Rapids. When Stanley went ahead on foot to talk with the Zinga chief, disaster struck again.

Frank Pocock, suffering from infected feet, demanded to be put aboard the lead canoe. Uledi, the Zanzibari steersman, had doubts about the rapids. He told Frank it was impossible to shoot the rapids and live. But Frank wouldn't believe him.

Three others of the crew backed up Uledi, saying the rapids were impassable. Frank laughed at them. White men, he said, would not be afraid to ride them.

Cannibal Country

It was a challenge Uledi could not resist. He would show Frank that black men feared death as little as whites. They would do it!

The canoe shot out of the shallows and was instantly swept into the current and overturned. Fighting for his life, Uledi struggled to the surface and grabbed at a submerged gunwale. Eight men managed to work their way out of the rapids. Frank Pocock was not one of them. His body was found eight days later down the Congo.

The Zanzibaris were disheartened by Frank's death. Now all the white men were dead except Stanley. If he died, what would become of them? Leaderless, they would perish in the great wilderness. They were hungry, tired, sick and demoralized. They told Stanley they would go no farther down the terrible river.

"I am as hungry as any of you," he replied. "I am so tired and sorry that I could lie down smiling and die. If you all leave me . . . I can then go to sleep forever. There are the beads, take them, do what you will. While you stay with me, I follow this river until I come to the point where it is known. If you do not stay with me, I still will cling to the river, and will die in it." He walked away, not looking back.

The Zanzibaris followed him. They would always follow him because they could not seem to help themselves. He had a magnetism they could not resist.

Through June and July they toiled over and around more rapids—mere skeletons of men—until they finally reached the last cataract at Isangila. The occasion had a peculiar effect on the brave Safeni.

"Ah, master!" he cried, rushing to Stanley. "We have reached the sea! We are home! We shall no more be tormented by empty stomachs and accursed savages! I shall run all the way to the sea to tell them we are coming!"

Whirling, he raced into the jungle. Only then did Stanley realize that his best man had cracked under the strain. Safeni had gone insane. They never saw him again.

On August 9, 1877, the safari limped into the town of Boma situated at the mouth of the Congo River. There they were greeted by a handful of Europeans and a cheering crowd of Africans. Their epic three-year trek across Africa had ended.

The cost had been steep. Three white men and more than 170 African members of the expedition had paid with their lives. But the geographical achievements had been worth the price. Stanley had surveyed Lakes Victoria and Tanganyika, discovered numerous other lakes and rivers, solved the mystery of the Lualaba, and explored the entire Congo River.

12. The Empire Builder

STANLEY returned to Europe in January, 1878. He badly needed a long rest. His stocky frame was debilitated, and though he had just turned 37, he looked nearly 50. Africa had taken its toll of him.

Doing his best to avoid banquets, interviews and crowds, he went to a Swiss resort to recuperate and write a book on his African trek called *Through the Dark Continent*. However, he soon discovered that he did not have the knack for resting. Without a job to do he felt bored to death. His restless energy had to be appeased, and so he began to lay plans for the founding of an empire in Africa.

He was convinced that all of humanity would be well served if he could infuse the civilization of Europe into the barbarism of Africa. Isolation was the trouble with Central Africa. For too many centuries that vast mysterious land had been left to its own primitive devices. Surely the enlightenment of commerce, culture and Christianity would help transform the African from his savage state, would eventually wipe out the oppression of ignorance, superstition, slavery and cruelty.

He took his scheme to develop the Congo to England and presented it to the government, but no one was interested. When he turned to influential British merchants, he found as little enthusiasm. They thought his ideas impractical, and some even charged him with acting like a buccaneer who put commerce before religion.

In November Stanley went to Brussels to talk to the Belgian king, Leopold II. This shrewd monarch was more than interested. He had already organized a committee known as *Comité d'Études du Haut Congo* for the development of the Congo area, and promptly put Stanley in full command of the operation.

He sailed for Zanzibar in January of 1879.

Collecting 70 Zanzibaris and Somalis, Stanley sailed back around Africa and arrived off the mouth of the Congo in August. There he made this entry in his diary: "Having been the first to explore this great river, I am to be the first who shall prove its utility to the world. I now debark my 70 Zanzibaris and Somalis for the purpose of beginning to civilize the Congo basin." Brave words—but they proved to be exceedingly hard to live up to.

The Empire Builder

His first job was to build a road around the lower Congo cataracts. There was the usual ovenlike heat, the millions of disease-bearing insects, the impenetrable jungles filled with multitudes of wild beasts and primitive tribesmen. And there was also a large collection of Europeans appointed by the committee to assist Stanley. At least that was how it appeared on paper. In reality the Europeans were more of a hindrance than a help.

As a rule, Stanley had little trouble in dealing with Africans. But trying to get along with white men who were more adventurers than idealists was a difficult task for a man of his temperament. He didn't understand them; they didn't understand him. They were appalled by the living conditions, the food, the lack of benefits and bonuses, the monumental chore of hammering a road out of a wilderness with sledge hammers. They quarreled, bickered, and demanded everything from free tobacco to a raise in pay. When Stanley ignored their complaints, some wrote enraged letters to the committee.

In spite of endless haggling, Stanley managed to push his road around the cataracts from Vivi to Isangila. It was 25 miles long and took one year to build at the cost of the lives of six white men and 22 Africans.

The road itself had no name, but it gave Stanley one that was to follow him to his grave: *Bula Matari*—Breaker of Rocks. He acquired it by showing the Zanzibaris how to swing a sledgehammer.

The Man from Africa

At one point a French explorer visited the camp, took a look at the work that was being done, and was stunned when he realized that Stanley had fewer than 100 men to help him. The Frenchman reckoned without Stanley's determination.

On May 1, 1881, Stanley established his third permanent station at Manyanga, and promptly came down with the most devastating fever he had ever experienced in Africa. For two harrowing weeks he was gravely ill. In a lucid moment he decided he was dying and called the Europeans and Africans to his tent to ask them to complete the job he had set out to do. He could hear them gathering around him, but they appeared to be only shadowy forms. When he tried to speak his final words he was unable to utter a sound. But he had to speak—had to tell them before it was too late! A rush of anguish gripped him and made him gasp, and suddenly he could speak. It was such a relief that he cried, "I am saved!" Then he sank into unconsciousness.

The next day, though he weighed only 100 pounds, he was on the way back to health.

In centipede fashion Bula Matari's company moved up the Congo with a chain of stations, making treaties with the tribesmen for land rights. All went well until an avaricious chief named Ngalyema decided to welsh on his agreement.

Ngalyema had been paid for his land rights, but he pretended he never had received the money. He sent a messenger to Stanley demanding a second payment.

The Empire Builder

When Stanley ignored this unreasonable demand, Ngalyema sent a messenger with a warning: pay or else. Stanley refused to be coerced.

The next day Ngalyema and his armed warriors tramped wrathfully into the camp and found it deserted—except for Stanley, who was sitting before his tent reading a book. Ngalyema felt ill at ease. He looked around suspiciously. Where were all of Bula Matari's men? Then he noticed a brass gong suspended by Stanley's tent, and he asked what was that strange object.

Stanley told him to beware of the gong because it contained powerful magic: to strike it would instantly summon a company of armed men to spring from the very earth.

Ngalyema wanted to see it work. He demanded that Stanley strike the magical object. Pretending great distress, Stanley gave the gong a mighty *bong*! Quickly Zanzibaris and Somalis armed with muskets bounded out of the surrounding grass and leaped down from the trees, all yelling like banshees. Ngalyema's startled warriors, seeing this armed horde sweeping toward them, threw away their spears and ran shrieking into the jungle.

The establishment of posts in the Congo area was a long, arduous task. By the summer of 1882 Stanley had built five stations along 440 miles of the river, had a steamer on the Upper Congo, two motor-powered crafts operating between Isangila and Manyanga, the road open to traffic between Vivi and Isangila, and Léopoldville completed. He also had found time to explore the Kwa River to discover and name Lake Leopold.

Returning to Europe in September of that year, he reported on the progress in the Congo and asked the committee to appoint competent European officers. He was tired of quarrelsome dandies and complaining incompetents. Taking with him the committee's promise to find and send him the best men available, he shipped for Africa at the end of the year.

What he discovered upon his arrival might well have made him give up.

The motor crafts were no longer operating on the Lower Congo; the local tribes were in a state of near revolt because of mishandling by the white officers in charge; and Léopoldville, which was the apple of his eye, was in deplorable condition.

He immediately set to work to bring order out of chaos and to restore harmony in his sprawling empire. And, surprisingly, he was successful.

A man named Callewart had been killed and decapitated at Kimpoko, the station near the head of Stanley Pool; Stanley had to find out why the Africans had cut off his head . . .

The officer in charge of the transport of a whaleboat from Vivi to Isangila wrote he would not attempt to carry the boat with only 58 men; Stanley had to round up more bearers for him . . .

The Empire Builder

The officer in command of Mayanga wrote that the officer in command of Vivi would not send him the supplies he requested; Stanley had to go there and resolve the matter...

Luksic, an Austrian marine officer stationed at Manyanga, committed suicide; Stanley had to see that he received a decent burial...

Ngalyema, recovered from his fright of the gong, wanted more money; Stanley had to pacify him...

So it went, day after day, month after month.

By the spring of 1884 Stanley's five-year project had reached what he felt was a happy conclusion. He had made over 400 separate treaties with tribesmen and had extended his patrol stations 1,400 miles up the Congo. There were two steamers on the Upper Congo and three on the Lower. There were roads and even a short railroad line. Traders and missionaries were entering the Congo basin and beginning to construct their outposts. In April of that year the United States officially recognized the newly developed land as a sovereign state, and other European countries soon followed suit. The territory was to be known as the Congo Free State.

Satisfied with the results of his labor, he made a voyage to America to become a naturalized citizen of the United States. Then, acting as technical adviser for his adopted country, he attended a conference in Berlin which was held by the statesmen of 13 European nations. The express purpose of the meeting was to divide Africa like a tasty pie. Stanley had thrown open the door on the Dark Continent, and now everyone, with the exception of the United States and a few others, wanted to rush in and cut themselves a slice of the virgin land.

13. The Region of Horror

A GREAT unrest was troubling the Sudan. For many years England, France and Egypt had been bickering over that vast sun-parched land which is south of Egypt and north of the Congo. Each wanted to govern the Sudan in its own manner and for its own interests without taking into consideration the fact the Sudanese wanted to govern themselves. The time for an uprising was ripe.

In 1882 one Mohammed Ahmed, known as the Mahdi (Messiah), led his fanatical Dervishes across the land in a bloody campaign to oust all foreign powers from Sudan. Within the next two years the Mahdist movement was surprisingly successful, with the Dervishes defeating the Anglo-Egyptian forces in seven decisive battles and capturing most of the key towns. The uprising culminated with the fall of Khartoum and with the death of its defender, General Charles Gordon, on January 25, 1885. The English and Egyptians withdrew from the Sudan, and the Mahdi established his empire on the isolation principle.

But there remained one small thorn in his side.

One of Gordon's most valued men was still holding the town of Wadelai in the southernmost province of Equatoria, 35 miles north of Lake Albert. This enigmatic European who called himself Emin Pasha was the governor of Equatoria, and he and his small force of faithful Nubian soldiers had been defending Wadelai successfully against the Dervishes for two and a half years before the news of his desperate plight reached the outside world.

The English public was immediately aroused. Something had to be done. A relief column should be sent to Equatoria immediately to bring Emin Pasha the weapons and supplies he so desperately needed.

But the nations involved were hesitant. Great Britain had abandoned the Sudan and did not wish to reenter at that time. France stated that she no longer had any interest in the Sudan. Egypt simply said it could not afford to finance a relief expedition. Thus, by the middle of 1886, it was apparent that the financing would have to be done by public subscription, and that a privately sponsored party would have to go to Emin's aid.

Sir William MacKinnon, who was in charge of the Emin Pasha relief committee, approached Stanley in October to seek his advice about a possible route from

The Region of Horror

the east coast of Africa to Equatoria. Stanley told him that for a moderate amount of cash there was only one route—via the Congo River. He then offered to lead the expedition.

Having given his advice and offer, he sailed for an American lecture tour. Thirteen days after he had started his tour he received a cable from MacKinnon: "Your plan and offer accepted. Authorities approve. Funds provided. Business urgent. Come promptly."

Stanley arrived in England on Christmas Eve and was informed that the relief committee had vetoed the Congo route; they wanted him to go by way of the Msalala-Unyoro route, starting from the east coast. He was willing.

A total of 21,000 pounds had been raised by the relief committee, and Stanley set to work with it. He ordered nearly 30,000 yards of cloth, 3,600 pounds of beads, one ton of brass, copper and iron wire, six tons of rice. Writing to his agent in Zanzibar, he asked for 600 bearers, 40 pack donkeys, ten riding asses, and a collapsible steel boat. The Egyptian Government sent 510 Remington rifles, 100,000 rounds of ammunition, and two tons of gunpowder to Zanzibar. A London arms house contributed 50 Winchester repeaters, and even a Maxim machine gun was thrown in.

Stanley received applications from men all over England who were eager to join the expedition. He finally settled on seven who had army experience and ranged in age from 25 to 43. They were: Lieutenant William Stairs, Sergeant William Bonny, John Troup (he had served with Stanley in the Congo), Major Edmund Barttelot, Captain Robert Nelson, Arthur Mounteney-Jephson (a relative of General Gordon), and James Jameson, a naturalist.

At the eleventh hour the committee informed Stanley of a sudden change in plans: He would take the Congo route after all. Stanley received this news with mixed feelings. He knew the Congo route was the surest way, but he had already arranged for reserve provisions to be stored along the east coast route. The last-minute decision to go up the Congo meant the expedition might have to live off the land.

He sailed for Egypt on January 21. In Alexandria he met Surgeon Thomas Parke of the Army Medical Corps, who was anxious to take part in the enterprise, and signed him on as medical officer. He then proceeded through the Suez Canal and the Red Sea, arriving in Zanzibar on February 22. Everything was in good order; men, supplies and pack animals were ready and waiting. But first Stanley had to see his old friend Tippu-Tib.

Tippu-Tib's Arabs had recently attacked and captured the Belgian station at later-day Stanleyville. If King Leopold decided to retake the station, Stanley's expedition would likely find itself caught in the midst of a war. Acting in Leopold's name, Stanley found a diplomatic way to sidestep this impending disaster: if Tippu-Tib would furnish men for the expedition, Stanley would have him appointed governor of the Stanley Falls district, which would place him in the employ of the Congo Free State. Leopold would still have his station; Tippu-Tib would also have it; and Stanley would have extra bearers, making everyone happy. The old slave trader agreed.

The expedition sailed for the Congo on February 24, 1887, a total force of 804 men: nine white men, 623 Zanzibaris, 62 Sudanese, 13 Somalis, and 97 of Tippu-Tib's Arabs. Stanley divided the Africans into companies and appointed one of his white officers in command of each company, cautioning them against using harsh treatment when dealing with their men.

All the officers agreed to his instructions. Unfortunately, Stanley did not know that Major Barttelot had a deep-rooted hatred for all men with dark skins.

The expedition disembarked at Banana at the mouths of the Congo on March 18 and immediately heard bad news. The steamer Stanley had intended to use as a transport had gone aground on a sandbar; famine was stalking the Congo; all the villages from Matadi to Stanley Pool had been abandoned; local bearers were not to be had at any price.

The white officers were greatly disheartened, but Stanley was used to this sort of trouble. Something was always going wrong on an African safari; you simply did the best you could. He found whaleboats for his men and supplies and moved up rapidly to the deserted Vivi, where they began the long march to Isangila.

A young adventurer named Herbert Ward met them on the road. He had been working in the Congo for a few years and was on his way home, but after talking with Stanley he decided to join the safari instead. Stanley was glad to have him.

Ill feeling between the Sudanese and Zanzibaris spread to local tribesmen as the column proceeded up the river. Without the reserve provisions, and with famine on the land, the scarcity of food quickly became a major problem. When the Zanzibaris began to steal food from the villagers, Stanley was kept busy pacifying irate chiefs.

On top of this trouble the bearers were starting to desert and disease soon crippled about 100 of them. Under these adverse conditions it wasn't long before the officers came to the conclusion that rescuing Emin Pasha was not the lark they had thought it would be. James Jameson told his wife in a letter that they had to march from 6 A.M. to 6 P.M. with seldom more than a 15-minute rest period all day. He also wrote that he and the other officers had had a few warm disagreements with Stanley—because Stanley did not know how to deal with English gentlemen.

A furious altercation occurred on May 20 when some Zanzibaris told Stanley they had bought food from a village and that Stairs and Jephson had taken it away from them. The two officers claimed the Zanzibaris had stolen the food. Hot words began to fly among the three white men. Stanley became so incensed that he offered to fight the two.

It did not come to fisticuffs, however, and after some general apologies the matter blew over. But from that

The Region of Horror

time on the relationship between Stanley and his officers was strained.

The expedition reached the village of Bolobo in May. Ward and Bonny were left there in charge of 129 sick Zanzibaris. Major Barttelot was placed in command of an escort to take Tippu-Tib's Arabs to Stanley Falls, and Stanley led the rest of his party to Yambuya, a village above the mouth of the Aruwimi River.

Yambuya was the jumping-off place. Whaleboats and power launches had to be abandoned, and the expedition would have to rely primarily on its weary feet. Yambuya was 500 miles west of Wadelai.

Stanley's plan was this: he, Stairs, Nelson, Jephson and Parke would take 383 men, with one-third of the supplies, and proceed to Lake Albert to meet Emin Pasha. They would be the advance guard. Barttelot, Jameson and Troup would remain at Yambuya with 130 men and two-thirds of the supplies, and Ward and Bonny would bring their 129 men up from Bolobo on the steamer *Stanley* and join the major at Yambuya. This would be the rear guard. Meanwhile Tippu-Tib had agreed to find 600 bearers and bring them to Yambuya. When he did, the rear guard would march with the remainder of the supplies and join the advance guard.

Before departing from Yambuya Stanley gave Barttelot a final word of warning regarding the management of the rear column.

"Your column may be ruined if you are not very

careful. Be tender and patient with your people, for they are as skittish as young colts. Still, it was with these people, or men like them, that I crossed Africa—followed the course of the Congo to the sea, and formed the Congo State."

The advance column marched out of Yambuya on June 28, 1887. A vast and awesome rain forest, a jungle which no white man ever had entered, waited for them like a towering enemy.

It was an abominable place. Stanley called it a "region of horrors" and compared it to a tomb. The soaring trees and the dense 15-foot high thickets dripped moisture. And it was always twilight; few blades of sunlight were able to penetrate the matted roof 200 feet overhead.

Hacking, shoving, stumbling over mazes of roots the size of elephants' legs, clawing through webbed creeper vines as large as fire hoses, the column probed deeper into the dark heart of the mysterious jungle.

Huge snakes were everywhere; ticks, ants, worms, slugs, mosquitoes armed with malaria, all added to the misery. Scratched and lacerated, the men's bleeding skins attracted hordes of flies. At night the mosquitoes had a feast.

For three weeks the advance column made a mere five miles a day through the jungle. By that time many of the Zanzibaris were gravely ill and Lieutenant Stairs had become a stretcher case. Stanley shipped his steel boat, the *Advance*, on the river and loaded the sick and much of the provisions into it and 11 large

The Region of Horror

canoes. The expedition now moved forward in two groups, one by water, the other by land.

On August 13, Stairs, having regained his health, took a scouting party across the river and was attacked by bushmen. Stanley heard a fusillade of shots and rushed his men to Stairs' aid. The scouting party was firing blindly into the brush at the unseen enemy, and Stairs was lying on the shore with an arrow in his chest.

While the troops beat off the attackers, Surgeon Parke drew the arrow from Stairs' chest and sucked the poison from the wound, which undoubtedly saved the young lieutenant's life.

Two days later Jephson, Parke and Nelson, along with the land section, managed to lose their way in the jungle and Stanley found himself stuck in camp. He had 29 men sick and eight with arrow wounds.

On August 21 the lost section found its way back to camp, and the advance column now consisted of 373 men, 57 of them sick. Then they slashed their way on until, one day, Stanley's servant came running and yelling from the river bank.

"Sir, Emin Pasha has arrived!"

"Emin Pasha!"

"Yes sir, I have seen him in a canoe. His red flag is hoisted up at the stern. It is quite true, sir!"

Stanley could hardly believe it. Yet a red flag meant an Egyptian flag! He rushed down to the river and found not Emin Pasha but an Arab slaver with nine Manyuema guards. It was a discouraging blow; wherever the slavers preyed, the tribesmen became openly hostile toward all strangers.

On September 17 they reached the slaver's settlement and Stanley left 56 of his sick in the care of Ugarrowwa, the slave trader. The Arab chief extracted a stiff payment for his clemency.

The following days of struggling through the endless jungle were like a nightmare to everyone. Stanley set up a small camp in a gloomy spot by the river on October 6 and left Nelson and 52 sick men there with 81 supply loads and ten canoes. The spot was referred to as "Starvation Camp No. 1." The rest of the expedition pushed on for Lake Albert.

There was no food in the land. They ate grubs, slugs, white ants, caterpillars and fungi. Malaria struck them. Ticks worked into their nostrils. Vermin crawled through their sodden clothes. Skin ulcers covered their bodies.

Reaching an Arab settlement at Ipoto on October 17, Stanley had to barter away some of his precious rifles and ammunition in order to obtain food for his starving men. A few days later Jephson and 40 Zanzibaris started back to Starvation Camp to bring up the others.

As they approached the silent camp they began to notice human skeletons along the way—a mere preview of the disaster that had occurred there. There was no sound except for the groans of two men dying in a hut. Nelson, a mere wisp of his former self, was sitting in an apathetic slump before his ragged tent. He had only five men left with him. The other 47 had starved to death.

Returning to Ipoto with Nelson, Jephson found that Stanley had already forged on with the main party, leaving Surgeon Parke behind with 26 sick men.

The expedition toiled on through the jungled creeper vines and tree-ferns for another two weeks, reaching the lush territory of Ibwiri in early November. The slavers had not visited this area and Stanley was able to make friends with the tribesmen and barter for food at reasonable prices. Then the advance guard sat down to its first real meal in two and a half months.

On November 14 Jephson and his men caught up to the main column, and Stanley made a head count. Of the 388 men who had entered the great forest in June, only 175 remained.

In order to fatten up his men and restore strength to their wasted bodies, Stanley held the safari at Ibwiri for two weeks. Then, on November 24, they set out on the last leg of the long trek to Lake Albert. Reaching a deserted Pygmy village on December 2, they were delighted to see that the conical huts were thatched with grass. One of the men climbed to the top of a hut and called down that he could see the grasslands of Equatoria in the distance.

Two days later the forest began to open on the beautiful panorama of a sunbathed grassy plain. With a rousing cheer of relief the officers and men rushed out of the dreaded rain forest into glorious daylight. It was the first time since they had left Yambuya, five months and 500 miles behind, that any of them had seen the sun in its splendid entirety.

14. The Way Back

VILLAGE after village stood deserted in the great savanna as the expedition trekked eastward. The tribesmen had gathered on the hills to watch the strange safari pass through their land. For four days they increased in numbers until there were well over a thousand of them, and the warriors were painted and armed for battle. On December 8 they began to shout war cries and wave their spears at the invaders.

Stanley selected a campsite on a hill and sent out a party of Zanzibaris to hold a talk with the warriors. But something went wrong. Suddenly the Zanzibaris opened fire and retreated in a panic. A great shout arose from the surrounding hills as the warriors surged forward to attack the camp.

Bowstrings twanged and bone-tipped arrows whistled in the air. Rifles crackled furiously in reply, repulsing the attack.

In the morning Stanley was appalled to see thousands of warriors on the green hills. And they were beginning to approach the camp. Then one of the Zanzibaris said he understood the warriors' dialect. Stanley used him as an interpreter to ask for a peace talk. After Stanley offered gifts of cloth and brass, the warriors retired.

On December 13, Stanley's men climbed out of the grasslands and found themselves on a broad plateau. Off in the east they could see the sweeping glimmer of Lake Albert.

The Zanzibaris were ecstatic with joy. Their arduous trek was over! But Stanley had grave misgivings as he studied the huge lake. Emin Pasha was supposed to meet him at Kibiro village on the east coast of Lake Albert. However, the safari had left the steel boat and canoes at Ipoto. Now there was no way for them to cross this vast lake. Supposedly Emin kept two steamers on the lake—but where were they?

After waiting for two days to see if one of Emin's steamers would make an appearance, Stanley decided to return to Ibwiri and build a stockade. From there he could send a party back for the steel boat and the canoes, and the advance column could wait in some comfort for Major Barttelot's rear guard to catch up.

It was an 18-day trek back to Ibwiri and much of the march was spent in fighting off the Wazamboni who were waiting for them in the savanna.

The Way Back

They constructed a sturdy stockade out of branches, mud and creeper vines, built barracks and storerooms inside it, and dug a moatlike ditch outside. Stanley named the post Fort Bodo. In the interim Stairs took a party back to Ipoto to fetch Nelson and Parke, the rest of the sick men, and the steel boat.

The fort was completed by late January 1888, and on February 7 Stairs, Parke and Nelson arrived with 15 sick Zanzibaris. The other 14 left at Ipoto had died. A week later Stanley fell ill and had to spend a month in bed racked with a peculiar and lingering gastric pain. During this time the fort was besieged by hordes of rats, fleas, mosquitoes and soldier ants, while patrols were sniped at by the ever-present Pygmies lurking in the bush.

By April 2 Stanley was on the road again, trekking back to the lake with Jephson, Parke, 126 men and the *Advance*. Captain Nelson was left in command of the fort with 60 men. Lieutenant Stairs had started downriver to see if he could discover what was holding up Barttelot's rear guard.

When Stanley's party reached the village of Kavalli on the great plateau on April 19, a letter from Emin Pasha was waiting.

Emin's letter said he had heard that a white man was in the territory, that he assumed it was Stanley, and that he was now looking for him along the lake. Stanley dispatched Jephson and a party of men in the *Advance* to find this man he had been trying to reach for over 13 months.

THE MAN FROM AFRICA

Jephson found Emin and returned with him aboard the small steamer *Khedive* to Stanley's camp on April 29. The excited Zanzibaris fired their rifles in the air while Stanley waited outside his tent to greet Emin. He was somewhat surprised to see a short, slight, bespectacled and bearded man wearing a red fez squarely on his gnomelike head step forward.

"I owe you a thousand thanks, Mr. Stanley. I really do not know how to express my thanks to you."

"Ah, you are Emin Pasha. Don't mention thanks, but come in and sit down. It is so dark out here we cannot see one another."

The next day Stanley gave Emin the ammunition he had brought with him, and the two men went aboard the steamer to discuss their plans. To Stanley, the man of action, there was only one obvious decision to make: how soon would Emin be ready to leave Equatoria?

But Emin was a man plagued by an indecisive nature. He could never quite make up his mind about what course he should take next in any matter, large or small. Now that he had ammunition and knew that more supplies were coming to him, he wondered if perhaps he should continue to try to hold the province for Egypt. The big problem on this score was that he doubted if he could still count on the complete loyalty of his officials and soldiers.

Stanley's opinion was that he should certainly get out of Central Africa while he had the opportunity, seeing that Egypt and England had abandoned him along with the Sudan. If, Stanley reasoned, Emin's provinces were situated within a reasonable distance of the sea, where he could receive the necessary supplies to hold his position, then it might be wise to stay in Equatoria.

"But here," he said, "surrounded as this lake is by powerful kings and warlike peoples on all sides, by such a vast forest on the west, and by fanatic followers of the Mahdi on the north, were I in your place I would not hesitate one moment what do to."

Still, Emin could not quite bring himself to make a decision. After mulling it over for a few days he announced to Stanley that he would leave it up to his people. If they wanted to leave, he would go; if they did not, he would stay. He wished that Stanley would return with him to Wadelai to help talk his soldiers into quitting Equatoria. But by this time Stanley was becoming too concerned over the prolonged absence of his rear guard to worry about Emin's irresolute soldiers. He instructed Jephson to go in his place, giving him a letter to read to the Sudanese troops.

It seemed strange to Stanley and Jephson that they should have to *induce* Emin's people into letting the expedition save their lives.

Stanley left for Fort Bodo with Parke and the Zanzibaris on May 24. That same day he made a geographical find that had been puzzling cartographers for hundreds of years. He saw a cluster of snow-capped mountains located near the equator. It was the Ruwenzori range, the legendary Mountains of the Moon. The highest peak was later to become known as Mount Stanley.

Lieutenant Stairs was waiting at Fort Bodo when Stanley arrived. He had backtracked through the forest as far as Ugarrowwa's settlement looking for Barttelot's rear guard, but without success. He had brought back 14 of the sick who had been left with the Arabs. The other 42 had died.

Stanley, wondering what had happened to the rear guard, decided to see for himself. He set out for Yambuya on June 16, taking with him 119 Zanzibaris and 100 Madi tribesmen who were loyal to Emin Pasha.

Though the jungle trail to Yambuya had been blazed the previous year, the safari had a brutal trek to endure. Reaching Ugarrowwa's settlement on July 13, they found that the slavers had abandoned their outpost and gone west. It was discouraging news. All of their portable food was now gone and they had counted on obtaining fresh provisions from the Arabs. By July 25 they were starving.

Nearly every man in the safari was the victim of some ghastly disease or ailment: huge tumors, fetid skin ulcers, skeletal debility, and chronic dysentery.

Bula Matari was not much better off than his men. He had had no meat of any kind for nearly a month, subsisting only on a Spartan diet of bananas and plantains. His muscles had become thin and flabby, reduced to mere cords and sinews; his limbs trembled violently at every step.

The safari came upon the westbound Arab slavers on August 11 and was able to get some fresh food and three canoes. They found three more canoes on the Aruwimi River. This was enough for Stanley to put his entire party on the water, for he was now down to 130 men.

Feverishly he drove his little flotilla down the Aruwimi, eager to reach Yambuya and discover what had happened to the long overdue rear guard. He had a foreboding that some terrible calamity must have occurred.

On the morning of August 17 the six canoes approached the village of Banalya, nearly 90 miles above Yambuya, and Stanley saw a stockade near the shore. A red flag bearing the white star and crescent of Egypt was floating on a staff over the palisade.

"It's the Major, boys!" Stanley cried out. "Pull away!"

Pulling rapidly into shore, Stanley saw Africans standing on the bank and called to them in Swahili, "Who are you?"

"We are Stanley's men," they responded.

Stanley jumped from his canoe and was greeted by William Bonny.

"Well, Bonny, how are you? Where is the Major? Sick, I suppose?"

"The Major is dead, sir," Bonny replied.

"Dead? Good God! How dead? Fever?"

The Man from Africa

"No sir. He was shot."

Stanley was stunned. "By whom?"

"By the Manyuema—Tippu-Tib's people."

"Good heavens! Well, where is Jameson?"

"At Stanley Falls."

"What on earth is he doing there?"

"He went to obtain more bearers."

"Well, where are the others—Ward and Troup?"

"Mr. Ward is at Bangala."

"Bangala!" Stanley was nonplussed. Bangala was 400 miles down the Congo!

"Yes sir, he is at Bangala, and Mr. Troup was invalided home some months ago."

Baffled and disgusted by the failure of his officers to carry out his orders, Stanley set about repairing the damage that had been done. The first step was to restore confidence in the miserable Zanzibaris of the rear guard. These men looked upon Bula Matari as their father and they brought their complaints and woes to him, telling him how unfairly they had been treated.

"Sit down, children," he said to them, "and let us talk this matter over quietly."

It was all they needed to bolster their spirits—someone to talk to them, to explain, to give them understanding instead of blows. *"Inshallah!"* they cried at the close of the meeting. They would follow him to Lake Albert . . . would follow him to the ends of the earth if he asked it of them.

15. The Last Trek

ON AUGUST 31, 1888, Stanley began his third trek through the great forest. With him went Bonny, 328 Zanzibari, Madi and Manyuema bearers, 25 guards, and 108 Manyuema chiefs, women and children.

There was the inevitable food shortage, the savages skulking in the dense foliage with their bows and arrows, and smallpox nearly decimated what was left of the Madis. By mid-October Pygmies and pox had killed 54 people.

They were caught by the rainy season and the jungle became a ghastly slough. On one day alone they had to ford 32 swollen streams. By the first week of December there was no food left and the safari was on the verge of collapse.

Somehow they struggled on, encouraged by Stanley's

booming voice: "Up, boys, up! Please God, we shall have plantains today!" And some days they did—when the scouts he sent out were successful in their foraging.

The safari stumbled into Fort Bodo on December 20. It was not a land of plenty. The three officers and 55 men had seen hard times. Pygmies had raided the fort's gardens of most of the vegetables and roving elephants had trampled what was left. For meat they had eaten Emin Pasha's donkeys, and when that supply was exhausted they had turned to fried ants.

Pygmy snipers had killed a few, and all were suffering from infected rat bites. Fort Bodo rats, it seems, had a taste for the ears, noses and cheeks of sleeping men. But their greatest concern was the lack of news regarding Emin and Jephson; seven months now, and not one word from them.

Stanley, plagued by the fear that some disaster had overtaken Emin and Jephson, abandoned Fort Bodo on December 22 and set out for Lake Albert. His total force now stood at 412. They were so hampered by sick and wounded that it took them 24 days to reach Kavalli.

The following day, January 11, 1889, Stanley received a letter from Jephson. Hastily he tore it open, scanned the penned lines, and groaned. The worst had happened. A rebellion had broken out in Equatoria: Emin's officials and soldiers had taken over Wadelai and made their governor a prisoner! Jephson said that *he* was allowed to go about freely, but that his movements were watched by the rebels. However, he was certain that he could escape, and would do so as soon as he heard from Stanley.

Stanley was puzzled by certain contradictory statements in Jephson's letter. In one place he said Emin was kept a close prisoner "unable to move hand or foot"; in another he said, "I trust the Pasha will be able to accompany me."

In his written reply Stanley told Jephson to "be wise, be quick, and waste no hour of time" in reaching Kavalli. He went on to say that he was ready to do anything to save Emin if the Pasha was *willing to be saved*. He concluded with—"Come; I am ready to lend him all my strength and wit to assist him. But this time there must be no hesitation, but positive yea or nay, and home we go."

Jephson reached Kavalli on February 6 and tried to explain to Stanley the confused situation in Equatoria; but the political affairs in that unhappy land were so interwoven with intrigue, deception, treachery and stupidity that no one could understand them. All of which did very little to soothe Stanley.

He dispatched a letter to Emin, giving him three choices: commandeer a steamer and come to Kavalli via the lake; make a march overland; or stay where he was and let Stanley come rescue him. He was quite prepared to adopt the latter course if necessary. In his usual way he had made friends with the neighboring chiefs, had consolidated 15 tribes into a binding confederacy, and could have raised 2,000 fighting men if he needed them.

His stormy ultimatum had the desired effect. On February 17 two steamers came across the lake and disembarked 60 Egyptians and their luggage. Emin Pasha had at last arrived.

Emin was as indecisive as ever. At first he wanted Stanley to wait while the rest of his people made their way out of Equatoria to join him in leaving Central Africa. Stanley agreed, and for the next month nearly 500 Egyptians (Nubians and Arabs of doubtful loyalty) dribbled into Kavalli.

Emin received encouraging news from Equatoria that many more of his people intended to join the expedition, but as March passed and none of them made an appearance, Stanley began to suspect that a plot to attack and raid his camp was afoot. Emin's officials and soldiers were obviously stalling for time. He sent a dispatch to them, giving fair warning that if they were not at Kavalli by April 10 he would march without them.

It was at this point that Emin changed his mind. He told Stanley he had decided to stay with his people.

"What people?" Stanley asked wearily.

"Why, with my soldiers."

Stanley then had to remind Emin that it was his own soldiers who had deposed him, made him a prisoner, and threatened to carry him to Khartoum and turn him over to the bloodthirsty Mahdi.

The Last Trek

His memory refreshed, Emin agreed that it would be unwise for him to remain in Equatoria. Yes, he would leave with Stanley—or so he thought at the moment. A little later one of his officers, Captain Casati, told him that in *his* opinion it was the governor's duty to stay in Equatoria.

Emin's resolution wavered like a reed in a wind. To stay or not to stay? He could not bring himself to a definite yes or no. By April 5 Stanley had reached the limit of his patience with the irresolute Emin and his unruly people. He *ordered* them to obey his commands on pain of death.

On April 10 the column filed out of camp and headed south. There were 1,500 people under Stanley's command: 230 Zanzibaris, 130 Manyuema, 550 men from the Kavalli plateau, and nearly 600 Egyptians. Three days out of Kavalli Stanley was taken seriously ill with a gastric disorder and the column came to a halt.

With Bula Matari out of action some of the Egyptian soldiers resorted to their old tricks of stealing weapons and ammunition and plotting to capture the expedition and turn it over to the Mahdi. Lieutenant Stairs apprehended 20 rebels who had tried to desert to the Mahdi, and Stanley lived up to his promise. He hanged the ringleader.

Stanley was on his feet by May 7, and the column was on the move again.

The long ungainly column plodded south for 350 miles, discovering Lake Albert Edward in June. Then it skirted the southernmost tip of Lake Victoria and proceeded east into the Unyamwezi territory, arriving at a new mission station in Usambiro on August 27. They rested at Usambiro for nearly three weeks, then swung south again, picking up the old caravan trail that Stanley had taken 18 years before in his search for Livingstone.

Turning east in October, they followed the trail to Mpwapwa, where the Germans had built an outpost. From that point on their homeward path was quite comfortable. Germany had made great strides in East Tanganyika since Stanley had led his last safari through that territory. Now the way was pegged with military and missionary stations and the isolated Germans greeted the column with great enthusiasm.

On November 30 they encountered a caravan which had been sent out by the relief committee to meet Stanley with fresh supplies. It was a trifle tardy, as the column was only four days from the coast.

Early on the morning of December 4, 1889, the column approached the outskirts of Bagamoyo. Stanley and Emin rode ahead on a pair of donkeys and halted in the village square. The great Indian Ocean spread before them, gleaming in the morning sun.

"There, Pasha," Stanley said. "We are home."

"Yes, thank God," Emin replied.

Had it been worth it? From the standpoint of personal achievement—one man's determination to pit himself against impossible odds and win—yes; but

The Last Trek

from the viewpoint of human life, no. The expedition had saved Emin and nearly 600 Egyptians (though we will never know if they actually *wanted* to be saved), but to do so it had lost over 600 people. This balance in human lives pretty well nullified the value of the expedition's original purpose to bring supplies to Emin Pasha, since he finally lost Equatoria.

Ten whites, 623 Zanzibaris, 62 Sudanese and 13 Somalis had started into Central Africa to save Emin. Six whites, 178 Zanzibaris, 12 Sudanese, and one lone Somali came out of Central Africa nearly three years later—a loss of 512 people. Add to this the large number of Madi, Manyuema and Wacusu bearers who died along the Aruwimi and the total was close to 650.

As an ironic aftermath, Emin returned to Central Africa in 1890, hoping to amass enough supporters to help him regain his old province in Equatoria. He did not find any allies—instead, some Arab chiefs found him. They slit Emin Pasha's throat from ear to ear.

16. "Enough"

"When a man returns home and finds for the moment nothing to struggle against, the vast resolve which has sustained him through a long and a difficult enterprise dies away, burning as it sinks in the heart; and thus the greatest successes are often accompanied by a peculiar melancholy."

Stanley made this notation in his *Autobiography*. It was a wistful thought. There was still much left to be done in Africa, but it would not be done by the man who for 20 years had made Africa a household word. Stanley was now nearly 50 and malaria had wasted his body and sapped his energy. He would never again set out to conquer a new world.

Most men would have been satisfied. Not so with Stanley. Having come into the world an unloved homeless waif, he had started out to justify his existence. He had thrown himself like a piledriver against the blank face of the world's indifference, determined to gain recognition and acclaim. And he had succeeded admirably. Now, 35 years later, he had fame and fortune. But was it enough? He did not think so. Something was missing. There was a void in his life which no amount of lionization could fill.

He found the answer in the one thing he had never stopped to look for: love.

Dorothy Tennant was a lady in the true sense of the word. Her father had been a Member of Parliament and her mother was a descendant of Oliver Cromwell. Miss Tennant had met and admired Stanley before he had gone on the Emin Pasha expedition, and after his return to England in 1890 their renewed friendship ripened into love. They were married in July of that year.

The Stanleys spent the first year of their marriage in travel—Switzerland, Italy, France and America—a sort of vacation-lecture tour. Then across the world to visit Australia, New Zealand and Tasmania. It was always the same wherever they traveled: people wanted to discuss Africa's problems with Stanley, and it soon became apparent to his wife that his old restlessness was returning. Even though wasted from fever, he wanted to be up and doing. Adventure was still in his blood and Africa was calling to him from over the oceans and continents.

It was a great worry for Dorothy Stanley. She feared that one more journey to the Dark Continent would

"Enough"

kill her ailing husband. And yet she realized that he could not exist in idleness; he had to be occupied, be absorbed in some vital work. She suggested that he run for Parliament and Stanley agreed to give it a try. They returned to England in 1892 and Stanley became the candidate for the Liberal-Unionist party.

It was an appalling mud-slinging election. The opposition slandered Stanley abominably, spreading vicious lies concerning his cruel treatment of the savages in Africa. One of the most prevalent tales was that Stanley had once thrown a little black baby into the Congo for the crocodiles to eat! Unfortunately there were enough gullible people who believed these lies and Stanley was defeated at the polls by a slim margin.

But this setback presented a new challenge to Stanley. Three years later he returned to the political battlefield and won the 1895 election.

Stanley was a far cry from the typical bombastic politician. On the night of his victory his enthusiastic supporters carried him triumphantly into the campaign hall, shouting, "Speech! Speech!"

In response, Stanley gave them what is probably the shortest acceptance speech in political history.

"Gentlemen," he said, "I thank you. And now, good night." And he went home with his wife!

He was not happy in Parliament. To his mind it was all talk and no action. He was quite content to retire from politics at the end of his term. Having no children of their own, the Stanleys adopted a little boy named Denzil. In 1899 they bought a small estate in Pirbright and moved to the country.

The estate was called Furze Hill and Stanley was delighted with it. There was a little lake which his wife named Stanley Pool; it was fed by a stream which they called the Congo, and nearby was a small wood which became the Aruwimi Forest. Stanley took a lively interest in building stone walls and wooden bridges for his miniature Africa.

He was knighted by the Crown that same year, thus becoming Sir Henry Morton Stanley, G.C.B. But recognition and awards no longer had any meaning to him. He was through with all that. He was nearly 60 now and his vitality had gone. He was content to work in his garden and write his *Autobiography*. He had a family and a home. He had found peace at last.

On April 17, 1904, he suffered a severe attack of pleurisy and had to be taken to London in an ambulance. His condition gradually worsened during the following three weeks, and on the night of May 9 he slipped into a delirium.

"Oh, I want to be free!" he suddenly cried. "I want to go—into the woods—to be free!"

The following morning when Big Ben began to sound four o'clock, Stanley opened his eyes with a look of wonderment.

"What is that?" he asked.

His wife told him it was the clock striking four.

"Four o'clock?" he said quietly. "How strange. So that is time! Strange."

"Enough"

Big Ben was just striking six A.M. when Dorothy Stanley held a cup to her husband's mouth. He pushed the cup gently aside and murmured, "Enough." It was his last word.

Perhaps Great Britain never did quite accept this enigmatic man who had forced her into a recognition of his vital existence. Even after his death the dissension remained. It was only right that he should have been buried in Westminster Abbey beside his old friend Dr. Livingstone. But the Dean of Westminster denied the right, asserting that Stanley had not achieved enough distinction in his lifetime to be buried in England's hallowed shrine.

So Stanley was buried in the village churchyard at Pirbright, and his wife had a huge granite monolith erected over his grave. It was 12 feet high, weighed six tons, and bore this inscription:

HENRY MORTON STANLEY
BULA MATARI
1841–1904
AFRICA

John Rowlands was at rest.

Acknowledgments and Bibliography

Cameron, Verney Lovett. *Across Africa*. Harper and Brothers, New York, 1877.

Clemens, Samuel. *Mark Twain's Speeches*. Harper and Brothers, London and New York, 1923.

Commager, Henry Steele. *The Blue and the Gray*. Bobbs-Merrill Co., New York, 1950.

Farwell, Byron. *The Man Who Presumed*. Henry Holt Co., New York, 1957.

Mounteney-Jephson, A. J. *Emin Pasha and the Rebellion at the Equator*. Charles Scribner's Sons, New York, 1890.

Stanley, Dorothy. *Autobiography of Sir Henry Morton Stanley* (unfinished by Stanley; completed and edited by his wife). Houghton Mifflin Co., Boston and New York, 1909.

Wassermann, Jacob. *Bula Matari*. Liveright, New York, 1933.

All of the following reference books were written by Henry Morton Stanley and were published simultaneously by Sampson Low, London:

How I Found Livingstone. Charles Scribner's Sons, New York, 1872.

Acknowledgments and Bibliography

Coomassie and Magdala. Harper and Brothers, New York, 1874.

Through the Dark Continent. Harper and Brothers, New York, 1878.

The Congo and the Founding of Its Free State. Harper and Brothers, New York, 1885.

In Darkest Africa. Charles Scribner's Sons, New York, 1890.

My Early Travels and Adventures in America and Asia. Charles Scribner's Sons, New York, 1895.

Index

Abyssinian war, 45–50
Advance, 128–29, 134, 135
Africa, 45–50, 51 ff., 88–90, 91 ff.
Ahmed, Mohammed. *See* Mahdi
Arabs, 58, 63–64, 98–100, 124–31, 138, 139, 144, 147
Arkansas, 27–28
Aruwimi River, 105, 127, 139, 147
Ashanti campaign, 88–90
Asmani, 57, 58, 66–67, 68
Autobiography, 149, 152

Bagamoyo, 57–58, 76–77, 92, 146
Banalya, 139–40
Bangala, 107–8, 140
Barcelona, 37–38
Barker, Fred, 92, 96
Barttelot, Maj. Edmund, 124–28, 134, 135, 138–40
Belgium, 114, 118
Bennett, James Gordon, 45, 49, 50
Bennett, James Gordon, Jr., 53–55, 73–74, 79, 84–85, 88, 92
Bolobo, 127
Bombay (guard), 57, 66
Bonny, Sgt. William, 123, 127, 139–40

Books, 85, 87, 113, 149, 152
Bravery, 52–53, 94–96, 108
British Association for the Advancement of Science, 82–83
Brooklyn, 38
Brynford, Wales, 19–20
Burton and Speke expedition, 55, 75

Cabin boy, 21–22
Camp Douglas, 35–37
Cannibal attacks, 101 ff.
Childhood, 13–25
Children, adopted, 65, 151–52
Citizenship, 119
Civil War, 28–33, 35–37, 38–40
Coffee, King (Kofi Karikari), 88–90
Comité d'Études du Haut Congo, 114, 115, 118
Confederate Army, 28–33, 35–36
Congo, 124 ff.
  Development of, 113–20
Congo River, 97–98, 105–12, 114–15, 123, 124
Cook, W. H., 40–41, 56

Index

Coomassie, 89–90
Cuba, 37

Denver, 40
Dervishes, 121 ff.

East Africa, 51–52
Egypt and Egyptians, 55–56, 121 ff., 136–37, 144, 145, 147
Emin Pasha, 122 ff., 134–38, 142–47
England and English, 13–21, 114, 150–53
  Abyssinian war, 45–50
  Ashanti campaign, 88–90
  Dislike of Stanley, 76–77, 82, 126, 151
  Emin Pasha, relief of, 121 ff., 137
  Livingstone search, 51–52, 76–77, 82–84
Equatoria, 122 ff., 133 ff., 142–45, 147
Europeans in Congo, 113 ff.
Exploration, 40–42, 55 ff., 75, 91–112, 118, 137–38

Fame, 79, 84 ff., 150
Family, 13–14, 19–20, 150–53
Farquhar, William, 56, 57, 61
Ffynnon Beuno, 13, 20
Fort Bodo, 135, 137–38
Fort Fisher, 39
France, 53–55, 88, 121–22
Francis, James, 14–17
Furze Hill, 152

Germany, 119, 146
Gold Coast, 88–90
Graham, Wilson, 43
Grant, Gen. Ulysses S., 29, 33

Hancock, Gen. Winfield S., 43
Hickok, Wild Bill, 44
Honors, 89, 152
How I Found Livingstone in Central Africa, 85

Ibwiri, 131, 134
Illnesses, 60–61, 64, 113, 116, 138–39, 150–51, 152–53
Indian campaigns, 43–44
Ingham, Major, 27–28
Inkisi Falls, 109
Ipoto, 130, 134, 135
Isangila, 115, 117–18, 125
Ituri territory, 93

Jameson, James, 124, 126, 127, 140
Jephson (Mounteney-Jephson), Arthur, 124–31, 135–36, 137, 142–43
Jerusalem, 56
Johnston, Gen. Albert S., 29, 32

Kalulu, 65, 87, 92, 96, 108
Kalulu Falls, 108
Kavalli, 142–45
Kingaru, 62–63
Kinshasa, 108
Kisangani, 105
Knighthood, 152
Kwa River, 118

Lady Alice, 93–96, 101, 103, 105 ff.
Lake Albert, 75, 96, 127, 130, 131, 134 ff., 143
Lake Albert Edward, 145
Lake Edward, 97
Lake Leopold, 118
Lake Tanganika, 51, 58, 75, 91, 97
Lake Victoria, 75, 91 ff.
Lectures, 82–83, 85, 133, 150
Leopold II, 114, 124–25
Léopoldville, 108, 118
Liverpool, 20–21
Livingstone, Dr. David, 51–52
  Death, 76, 88, 90, 91
  Meeting with Stanley, 69, 71 ff.
  Search for, 55–77, 79–84
Livingstone Falls, 108

INDEX

Livingstone search, 55 ff.
  Authenticity attacked, 79–84
  Bearers, 57, 58, 60, 61, 64–67
  Costs, 55, 56–57
  Distance traveled, 77
  Hardships, 59–61, 67, 77
  Meeting with Livingstone, 69, 71 ff.
  Members, 56, 57, 58
  Revolt by bearers, 66–67
  Supplies, 57, 59, 60
Livingstone Search and Relief expedition, 76–77
London *Daily Telegraph*, 91–92
Lualaka River, 74, 75, 83, 97–100, 101–5, 107
Lualaka River expedition, 91–100, 101–12

MacKinnon, Sir William, 122–23
Madi bearers, 138, 141
Magdala, Battle of, 46–49
Mahdi (Mohammed Ahmed), 121 ff., 137, 144–45
Manyuema, 67, 71 ff., 140, 141
Marriage, 150–53
Massassa Rapids, 110–11
Matadi, 125
Minambo, Chief, 63–64, 76
Minnesota, U.S.S., 38–40
Missionaries, 114, 119, 146
Missouri Democrat, 43
Mitumba, 101 ff.
Mombiti, 93
Mount Stanley, 138
Mountains of the Moon, 138
Mounteney-Jephson, Arthur. *See* Jephson, Arthur
Mowa tribe, 109–10
Msalala-Ungoro route, 123
My Kalulu, 87

Napier, Sir Robert, 46–50
Nelson, Capt. Robert, 124, 127, 129 ff., 135
New Orleans, 23–24
New York, 38, 45–46

New York *Herald*, 45, 49, 50, 52 ff., 72–74, 79, 80, 84–85, 92
Ngalyema, Chief, 116–17, 119
Nightingale, Florence, 85
Nile River, 51, 71, 74, 97
Noe, Louis, 40, 41–42, 56, 87
North Atlantic Blockading Squadron, 38–40
Nyangwe, 99, 103, 106

Omaha, 40, 41
Owen, Maria, 20
Owen, Mary, 13, 20
Owen, Moses, 19, 20
Owen, Tom, 20

Palestine, 56
Paris, 53–55, 88
Parke, Thomas, 124, 127, 129, 131, 135
Parliament, Member of, 151
Pocock, Edward, 92
Pocock, Frank, 92, 96, 98–99, 103, 107, 110–11
Price, Dick, 13–14
Prospecting, 44
Pygmies, 131, 135, 141, 142

Railroad in Congo, 119
Rawlinson, Sir Henry, 82
Reporter, 39, 40, 42, 43 ff., 90
Resourcefulness, 62–63, 96–97, 103, 117
Roadbuilding, 115, 119
Roberts, Willie, 15–16
Rowlands, Grandfather, 19
Rowlands, John (Henry M. Stanley), 13–25
Royal Geographical Society, 51, 52, 76–77, 82–84
Ruwenzori Range, 137–38

Safeni, 94–96, 112
Seaman, 21–22, 37–40
Selim, 56, 57, 64
Shaw, John, 57, 61, 64–65

Index

Shiloh, Battle of, 29–33
6th Arkansas Regiment, 29–33
Slave trade, African, 99, 129–30, 131, 138, 139
Slavery, U.S., 27–28
Smyrna, 41–42
Somali porters, 114, 125
Spain, 37–38, 52–53, 88
Speake, James, 24
St. Asaph Union Workhouse, 14–17
Stairs, Lt. William, 123–29, 135, 138, 145
Stanley, 127
Stanley, Denzil, 152
Stanley, Dorothy Tennant, 150–53
Stanley, Henry Morton (foster father), 23–25, 27, 37
Stanley Falls, 108, 124, 127
Stanley Pool, 108, 125
Stanleyville, 105, 124–25
Starvation Camp, 130–31
Sudan, 121 ff.
Suez, 46, 49
Suez Canal, 55

Tabora, 63–65, 76
Tanganyika, 51, 61–63, 71 ff., 88, 91, 97, 146
Theodore, King, 45, 47–49
Through the Dark Continent, 113
Tippu-Tib, 99–100, 101, 103, 124–25, 127, 140
Trading posts, Congo, 117–19, 124–25
Troup, John, 123–24, 127, 140
Turkey, 41–42, 56
Twain, Mark, 86

Ugarrowwa, 138
Ujiji, 58, 63, 65, 67–69, 71 ff., 97

Uledi, 110–11
Union Army, 29 ff., 36–37
United States Navy, 38–40
Unyanyembe territory, 63 ff., 75
Usambiro, 146

Valencia, 52–53
Victoria, Queen, 84
Victoria Nyanza, 75, 91 ff.
Vinya-Njara tribe, 104
Vivi, 115, 118–19, 125

Wadelai, 122, 137, 142 ff.
Waganda tribe, 96–97
Wales, 13–20
Wane-Mpungu tribe, 104–5
War prisoner, 35–37
War reporting, 39, 45–50, 52, 53, 88–90
Ward, Herbert, 125–26, 127, 140
Wavuma tribe, 96–97
Wazamboni tribe, 133–34
West Africa, 88–90
Western expedition, 40–41
Westminster Abbey, 91, 153
White Nile, 51, 71, 74
Windermere, 22
Wolseley, Gen., 88, 90
Workhouse, St. Asaph Union, 14–17

Yambuya, 127–28, 138
Youth, 21–24

Zanzibar, 56–57, 77–78, 123, 124
Zanzibari porters, 52, 57, 64–67, 93 ff., 103 ff., 123 ff., 133 ff., 137–38, 140
Zinga Rapids, 110–11
Zula, 46, 49

About the Author

When Robert Edmond Alter died on May 26, 1966, he left behind him not only the image of a vital man taken long before his time but a body of literature in which he made people and history pulse with life. His demand for historic validity, accuracy of detail and an absorbing style never wavered.

Born in San Francisco, Mr. Alter left home for a short turn as an itinerant citrus picker. After one year of college he traveled throughout the United States and Canada, working his way as a farmhand, construction worker, punch-press operator and movie extra. After being discharged from the Army he began to write and became the author of nine books and many short stories and articles before he died in Altadena, California, at the age of 41.

www.ingramcontent.com/pod-product-compliance
Lightning Source LLC
LaVergne TN
LVHW041625070426
835507LV00008B/453